# PARENTING THE GREATS

Teaching Your Children To Stand
Out In Their Christianity

KEVIN BUTLER

Printed in the United States of America

First Printing 2014

ISBN-13: 978-1493640867

ISBN-10: 1493640860

# DEDICATION

This book is dedicated to my own Greats. I pray that I keep the truths of this book as examples to you all and that you become what God desires you to be.

# CONTENTS

# ACKNOWLEDGEMENTS

There are so many people who have been a part of this writing project. While I can't name them all here, there are some that are due to be on this page. First, I want to thank my wife and kids. They make my life a blessed one.

I also want to thank the Beta Team for this book. This team consisted of Robin Moore, Jennifer Disney, Nancy and Rebecca Blom, Lisa Jones, Megan Reed, Michelle Weitzel, and my mother, Melissa Kyle. I can't thank you enough for all the time, input, direction, and editing you all have sacrificed to make this book the best it can be. I am a blessed and better writer because of you all.

I want to thank our family photographer, Jennifer Pitts. All photos in this book are printed by her permission. I want to also thank my church family. They are my biggest cheerleaders and encouragers.

I want to give a special thanks to author, Amy Parker who spent many hours away from the writing of her own book just to pass along her knowledge to a newbie. I can't thank you enough and I can't wait to pass it on.

# CHAPTER 1
## It's OK, You Can Drink After Me.

**"If you don't know what you're doing, it's best to do it quickly." – Jase Robertson**

Before we embark on this journey together, I need to draw some clear guidelines. I mean, I don't even know you, and you may know little about me. It's like the guy in the booth next to you at the restaurant offering to share his beverage with you. By the way, I wouldn't take strangers up on such offers.

Besides having a bus load of kids, what would qualify me to teach you something about Christian parenting? It would be awkward to share a book together as strangers, right? That's just weird. And, I don't want to be the weird guy. So, let me start by clarifying my idea of *Parenting the Greats*.

My overall desire, as a parent, has always been to raise my children to become people of greatness. But, somewhere down the parenting road, I stumbled off the pavement as to what true greatness really means. Unknowingly I had accepted the culture's view of greatness for my children. Throughout a number of events, God changed my views on what greatness truly means and He helped me to narrow down 10 things which I should raise my children to do well. I'm here now to share with you what I've learned.

When you observe our culture, it's evident that our children simply want to fit in to a normalcy which is rather, well... normal. But, is this best for our kids? If we allow our children to simply be normal then *what* about them as a person would be great? How would they stand out for God?

We can all list many ways our children can become people of greatness in our society, but what is greatness according to God? I believe I've found the answer.

Now, I'm not talking about raising some holy-rolling breed of children bent on building a sinless and dust free utopia. I'm talking about raising people who are not afraid to be different from the crowd. We need the next generation of Christians to be people who will stand up for their godly morals and convictions, even if their friends, coworkers, or spouses disagree.

But, do I really know what I'm writing about? Just what makes me qualified to write this book? When it comes to qualifications, I have three.

**Qualification #1: I come from a broken home.**

I smile at some of the odd moments from my childhood which are lodged in my memory. I remember the pet rabbit my parents bought me for my fifth Easter. I remember waiting patiently for this Easter rabbit to lay those huge chocolate eggs wrapped in shiny wrappers. I envisioned becoming the Willy Wonka of my Kindergarten class. Yet, before I could acquire a ridiculously flamboyant Porter Wagner type suit, my dreams of a chocolate monopoly melted away when my rabbit escaped into our neighbor's garden and was fatally wounded in action.

R.I.P. Mr. Snuggles, you are missed.

Others memories are even more painful. There is one memory in particular that I'm sure to carry around until my mind ceases to function. It's a very personal event which would forever change my life's course and eventually how I would be skilled as a father. Until now, I've never shared with anyone all the details I remember of this event, so: here it goes...

I remember this particular evening being routine, until I heard screams from my mother followed by yelling from my father. By the time I ran in to my parents' bedroom, my father was frantically unzipping his suitcase and beginning to violently throw his clothes inside. For some odd reason, I remember the color of the suitcase. It was olive green. My father grabbed the handle of what was now all his belongings and stomped his way to the front door. I ran with all the speed that my seven-year-old-legs would provide, and was able to catch up with him just as he was turning the front doorknob.

I lunged at the closest leg I could grab and quickly asked, "Daddy, where are you going?"

He stopped rotating the doorknob, gently took one knee, and looked me square in the eyes. Never before had I seen my father's eyes with such a reddening glaze. He then spoke, "Son, I can no longer live here. I have to leave. You are now the man of the house."

With that, my father stepped through the door frame, closed the door behind him, and left a seven-year-old boy and a wife who was seven months pregnant. Only years later would I begin to understand the reason for my parents' divorce. While my father and I had – what I thought was – a normal every-other-weekend relationship, I always felt as though something was missing in my life.

Today as a parent and reflecting back on that evening, there were two essential items I, as a child, needed from my father. What is amazing is the ongoing need of these two items in my life even as a grown man today. Number one, I needed my father to be a good example of love. Number two, I needed my father to be an example of great integrity. Standing there as a small child and watching my father peel out of the driveway, I hungered from then on for an example of great love and integrity.

An unnecessary burden was placed on a seven-year-old boy who could not possibly be the *man* of the house, even though he was told he had to be. A heavier burden was placed on a young pregnant mother. For the first time, our home was without a leader. The delinquent bills and heartbreaking pain would quickly and inevitably overtake our broken family.

This broken-home lifestyle would eventually challenge me to become a great dad. A dad who would provide for his children the two things I longed for as a child, great love and integrity. While it may seem as if I've painted an evil picture of my father, years later God would reconcile our relationship.

As a Christian, I must confess: these two qualities, love and integrity, are my favorite characteristics about God. What can compare to God's love for humans? Nothing! What degrading words can be spoken to refute God's great integrity? None! Often, I have young parents ask, "What are the qualities we need to be good parents?"

If I were to sum up the definition of a good parent in two words, they would be the words: love and integrity. If this is true, and I believe it is, then good parents wanting to be great parents must turn to the greatest example of love and integrity. Now, I wonder where one would find such a person that displayed the ultimate form of love for his children? One that displays the greatest example of pure, never-changing integrity? Well, we should look no further than to God Himself. And really, is there a greater love than God's love for humanity? If so, one would have to meet some very high standards. Besides this question, we should inquire, "Is it right to even think of God as the great parent of humanity?" This question will be answered in great detail later in this book, but chew on that question for now.

**Qualification #2: I only *has* a high school education.**

That's right. No need to worry about big words and incomprehensible (one of only two big words in the book) definitions from me. I'm just the average guy you would see at the grocery store standing in the checkout line trying to avoid the marked down chocolate bars.

One of the cursed strands of DNA I seemed to have passed on to my children is my overly chubby cheeks (facial cheeks, not the other set). You can spot a Tennessee Butler from a mile away. People who meet my children for the first time make the same statement to me, "Yep, those are your kids." As if this was in question?!

I can't help the fact that I have five pounds of jaw. And so, the genetic legacy continues throughout another generation. Why? Because my children were made in the image of my wife and I. But these images are not only transposed in physical traits but also in physiological traits, such as emotions and temperaments.

So, where does God come into all this parental-role-modeling stuff? Well, just like my children inherited my chubby cheeks, humans also inherited core qualities from God. The Bible reveals a very deep truth when it records God speaking in the book of Genesis. Within the first five verses of the Bible, we get a small glimpse of the heart of God as our great parental example. It would be well worth a read.

I decided years ago to turn to the Bible for my understanding and search for parental wisdom. The foundation for raising great godly children is there. I've lived the research for you and have written about my experiences in this book. The ten life-qualities which I strive to teach my children were all derived from God's Word.

A great fear of mine, while writing this book, is that you will finish reading it, place it on a shelf, and proceed to practice your parental duties exactly the same as you did before. There is a great danger in having the knowledge to change yet never applying that knowledge. When you do this, you never transform your knowledge into wisdom. And I want you to be a wise parent. Let me give you a clear example of having knowledge but not applying it to your life.

One weekend my family and I were at our local park when I noticed a father throwing ball with his son. As we got closer to this father and son, I could hear the dad giving instructions to his son on how to throw a curve ball. The young boy was listening intently with both ears poking out from under the rim of his loose ball cap. The boy's glove was visibly new, and you could sense this would be his first season of playing organized ball.

The dad instructed the boy on how to properly hold the ball in his hand, where to place his fingers to give the correct rotation and spin, what type of speed to project, and how to perform a flawless rocker-step. It was a good lesson. I learned a lot about how to throw a curve ball.

After the dad was done instructing his child he said, "Now, let me show you how to do it!"

The boy and father walked several paces away from each other, reminding me of a scene from an old western gunfight. The boy squatted down to play the catcher as dad took the imaginary mound. After such good instructions from the father, I decided to watch the performance.

He threw the first pitch, which missed his boy's glove by 20 feet! After the second pitch, I started looking for my wife and children in fear of them being hit.

After the third pitch, I wanted to move my car! As a dad, this was comical to me. This man had given great, even proper instructions to his son but could not perform the act himself.

Then the Lord spoke to my heart. I thought about how many times I have given clear, biblical instructions to my children, and yet I could not perform the act myself because of my spiritual weakness.

While these are the types of truths I will be sharing with you in our journey together, I don't want your journey to end when this book does. I want you to apply the knowledge you will receive in this book and transform this knowledge into a personal wisdom. Adopt these truths to your life and pass it on. This book is simply my way of a real, practical, and biblical parenting style. However, it's still up to you to apply the truths found here in this book.

### Qualification #3: I have children and children and children and children.

At the time of writing this book, my wife and I have seven children. I am thirty-seven years old; my wife is thirty-one. Yes, we've been busy, and there is a lot more work to be done! It's not that we are in a race against the Duggers, but rather, we enjoy children. My wife loves the entire process of pregnancy. And for me, it's amazing to see our children grow to become their own persons. The way they develop at such a rapid pace, the way they soak in knowledge like a sponge soaks in bath water, it's the greatest feeling in the world to know you have the task of shaping and molding humans. It's good just to be called a parent.

I write this book as a parent. I am not a pediatrician nor a child psychiatrist. I'm just a dad times seven. However, by the time you read this book, that number may be outdated.

In this journey together I will share biblical ways to raise children, not to be normal or average, but to be great and genuine in their faith. If you want greatness for your child, then journey with me. I personally invite you.

So, my qualifications: I had no great example, I have no higher education, and I don't know when to stop reproducing but I have dedicated my life to the study of God's Word and have discovered a think or to about Parenting. And now that you know me a little better, it's OK, you can drink after me.  : )

# Chapter Recap

**DO:**

- Read the rest of this book.
- Share the truths of this book with others.
- Take the time to implement the truths of this book into your parenting skills.

**DO NOT:**

- Throw this book in the trash, especially if you are reading this as an ebook.
- Ignore crosswalk signs.
- Read this book while showering.
- Put hand soap in a dishwashing machine. Trust me on this.

# CHAPTER 2
## Great in Their <u>Awareness</u>

**"Our View Of Greatness Is Greatly Flawed."**

If we were honest with ourselves, all parents would admit the hard truth: we all have problems with our parenting. None of us have the market on this parenting adventure. For me, I had to trace my parenting mistakes all the way back to my young teenage years. In those weird years of my life, I unknowingly formed a wrong understanding of what it means to be great. I remember that it all started with a basketball game.

The hardwood seemed as if it was acoustically tuned only to his sneakers. All other sounds dissolved as I watched him. He moved effortlessly, almost unnaturally. It seemed as if his skills were years above any competition on the court. He appeared to have an expression of laughter on his face as he weaved through opponents. The ball seemed to take on another form in his hands. It was like watching a well-timed dance routine. No one could stop this man. And then... he jumped, tongue hanging out. From the force of his momentum, his red jersey spread out behind him like a cape.

I remember seeing the thousands of flashes from

the cameras in the crowd. As a teenager, it was as if time had stopped as I watched this man perform what seemed like miracles through my television screen. The number twenty-three, showing on his chest as he hung from the rim.

For all you basketball nuts, I mean fans, you have already figured out the name of this man. Michael Jordan. Man, he was great! I remember wanting to be great just like Mike, not so much in basketball, but in my favorite sport called football.

As I grew older I realized a hard truth: I was good at football but not great. This realization would led to a feeling of defeat. As I turned to God's Word for my understanding of how to parent my children, I began to see that God's definition of greatness didn't line up with mine. I began to ask myself some honest questions. Is great talent all that's required to be a great person? Is being great at something... anything... good enough? According to God, my definition of greatness was a worldly understanding. I suppose it may depend entirely on whom you ask. Maybe that's the problem I had. I was asking the wrong people.

I guess I should begin by telling you how the idea for this book came about. My oldest son, Brice, loves baseball more than bacon. And let me tell you, he must really love baseball. There is something about bacon, which attacks most males, both young and old. I'm convinced if schoolbooks were made with bacon-scented paper, all young boys would make straight A's and most men would return to college.

On the field, he seems to play the game with the same expression of enjoyment that I remember seeing on Michael Jordan's face. Brice studies the game. He has all the MLB players' stats memorized. He awakes in the mornings searching for his glove. Did I mention Brice loves baseball?

One night while driving home from a late night practice, I told Brice, "Son, you practiced the best I've ever seen you practice. You have a great heart to play baseball, and if you keep your love for the game, you may even play in the Majors one day!"

This statement of encouragement seemed not to even register with Brice. He just sat there staring out the car window. He was quiet, too quiet. The cold air blowing from the car vents seemed to be the only thing he was feeling, and then he spoke the very words, which began the journey of this book. "Dad, I don't know if I want to be a baseball player when I grow up."

I was momentarily awestruck, but curiosity quickly began to take over. What would make a twelve-year-old boy, with an obvious addiction to baseball, not desire to be the greatest at the very sport he loves?

I finally spoke with the most intellectual response I could muster, "Huh?"

"Well, you've always told me that God has great plans for me. Right?"

"Yes, son. That's true."

"Well, what if His plans aren't for me to play baseball? I don't want to spend my life being great at something God doesn't want me to do."

Have you ever had those moments where your child threw down more logic in a conversation than you could have thought up? I found myself holding in my mind two distinct emotions:

**I felt pride.**

I was proud of my son for thinking such deep spiritual thoughts and then articulating them in a way that brought me conviction.

**I felt shame.**

What had happened to me? Why was my son relaying more spiritual insights than I? I am a preacher for Heaven's sake!

21

I realized at that very moment, I had lost my focus of what greatness truly means. I also realized I couldn't be the only parent sitting in this boat of confusion. I needed to discover for myself what it really means for my children to be great in God's eyes, and then I must share this newfound knowledge with other parents. You see, I quickly realized I had been following the culture's definition of greatness.

It doesn't take a genius to figure out what our culture defines as greatness. Somehow this warped view of greatness had clung to me like a dryer sheet clinging to the inside of my dress pants. Look around for yourself and you'll discover the reality of this danger. I'm writing of the danger of a warped view and not the danger of dryer sheets clinging to my pants. However, if there is a danger of dryer sheets clinging to a person's pants, for goodness' sake, please email me. I don't want to go out like that!

The youth today are bombarded with advertisements of what greatness means to our culture. The right clothing will make you great. The right athletic skills will make you great. The right college degree will make you great. The right musical talent will make you great. The right equipment will make you great. Our children's heroes are today's celebrities and no longer we parents. Our country is no doubt the leading producer of entertainment and education that is focused on talent and popularity.

But where did we, as Christian parents, get off track on our view of greatness? Did generations before us also have this same warped view of greatness? Where did it all begin? To find the answers, I had to look to a time long before America was even a country.

It seems as if missing the mark on a Godly definition of greatness is not just a modern day dilemma. As a Christian, I turned to the Bible to see if there were any examples of parents raising their children to be great at worldly things.

I was shocked at the many examples of parents in the Bible who found themselves off track with God's plan for their children.

The account of Jacob and Esau's upbringing shows evidence that even in the Bible, parents often struggled with raising their children to be Go-Getters for God. Somehow Jacob and Esau's parents had decided to raise each son in an entirely different way.

This account is found in the book of Genesis Chapter 25. Jacob and Esau's mother, Rebekah, was given a word from the Lord concerning these twins in her womb. In Verse 23 God tells this new mother that two nations will be brought about through these two babies. Can you imagine receiving a word like this from God? A clear prophecy that the children you are about to birth with will one day become the leaders of two great nations?

I'm a people watcher. I like to study all the different mannerisms and expressions of others, all while they have no idea I'm watching. I'm intrigued by the way they interact with others and by the way they converse.

At this moment, I'm sitting in a coffeehouse on my lunch adventure, sipping, typing, and watching. The workers are busy mixing. There's a couple talking about selling their home and the growing list of things to fix before the house can be put on the market. Just to my left is a man who apparently came just to enjoy the free Wi-Fi. The rest of the place seems to be scattered with local college students. Yes, I have headphones on.

Then there's the guy to my right... oh gosh... he just saw me looking at him. Now he's staring right at me. Man, he's still looking. Here's a crazy thought: What if he is also a writer who's putting me in his book at this very moment? Sorry, too much coffee so let me jump to the point.

Some evenings I work late hours and come home to find my children asleep in bed. Sometimes I will get a chair, sit down, and watch them sleep. They are beautifully quiet and motionless. I rarely get to see them when they are simply still. I can watch them and observe their facial features without worry of them noticing or shying away. While I observe them peacefully sleeping, I think about how they were formed in their mother's womb.

I think about how God shaped and molded them into who they are today. I dream about who they will become and the blessings they will get to be a part of.

I wonder what pains and trials they will have to endure for being Stand-Up Christians for God. I pray over their sleeping bodies and I pray for their future spouses. A thought just struck me: when they read this book, this part will really creep them out.

But there is one thing I would love to receive from the Lord. A prophecy like Rebekah's. A prophecy about who my children will grow up to be. As a parent wouldn't that be amazing to know ahead of time - how they will eventually turn out? Wouldn't that make parenting, well, easier? Probably not. I have big dreams and ambitions for my children but that doesn't make the parenting road any smoother.

I can't imagine how Isaac and Rebekah felt when they were told about the future of their babies. You would think these parents would have it all together, right? They are, after all, responsible for raising these boys to be the leaders of two great nations. However, we find that Isaac and Rebekah struggled with bringing out the greatness in these twins.

If you read the biblical account of Jacob and Esau's youth, you will quickly discover that their parents had trouble with teaching these young men how to do great things for God.

According to the Bible, Rebekah invested her parenting into the life of Jacob while Isaac cared only for Esau. This would mean that Isaac and Rebekah raised these boys almost independently from each other. The Bible later records Rebekah "cooking up" a plot to help Jacob in deceiving his own father while on his deathbed. She knew her husband couldn't see well, so she and Jacob took advantage of this. Sad. So, we find that Isaac and Rebekah were not exactly what we could call models of godly parenting.

It seems that even parents in the Bible had difficulty in raising their children to become people of greatness. There are many more examples we will observe through our journey together, but this is just one instance, which proves that parents have always had difficulty in raising children to do great things for God. While there are several examples of failed parenting in the Bible, there are even more biblical examples of parents training up a child in the correct way.

So, maybe all parents need are some guidance, tips, hints, and humor to help focus their parenting on the things that matter the most to God. Maybe you're a parent just like me who viewed a sports star as a man of greatness, even though I'd never met him. Just like I wanted to be like Mike, today's children want so badly to be like others they see in the spotlight.

Unfortunately, we often feed this unhealthy appetite in our children. We do this sometimes unknowingly, even in the teaching of our religion. Let's spend the next couple of chapters looking at real-life examples of how we teach our children the wrong type of greatness.

# Chapter Recap

**DO:**

- Be consistent in your childrearing with each child.
- Ask yourself this question, "What would I consider greatness to look like in my child?"
- Take time to pray today and ask God to reveal what greatness means to Him.

**DO NOT:**

- Love one child more than the other.
- Put your parental responsibilities off on your spouse.
- Stalk people inside of a coffeehouse.

# CHAPTER 3
# Great in Their Biblical Understanding

### "Be Sure to Scare The Noah Out of Them."

Fudge popsicles are a child's dream and a carpet's worst nightmare. One evening, my family and I were relaxing at home, eating fudge popsicles. Perfect night, right? It was until... our 18-month-old son, Truett, came to me holding out his dirty hands.

I realize this is only chapter three, and we haven't really bonded yet, but I'm going to throw this in for free. Here's your first parenting tip: If your child will not even smell his own hands, you better know something has gone terribly wrong! Whatever you do, DO NOT lick before you smell! My gut told me, "That's not melted chocolate!" But for some reason my brain said, "Oh, look at all that wasted fudge." And my gut and my nose were right that night. Unfortunately, my brain blocked out that message until it was too late. Even though it looked like melted fudge, it was definitely not!

In the same light, as dimly as it shines, we should never raise our children in a way which looks right to us, but smells terrible to God. Even our basic, biblical teachings have been formed and shaped by our culture to present God in a casual way.

Most of the biblical stories we tell our children do them more harm than good. That's right! If we're not careful, our children will grow up with a weird view of God. Later in life, they will become confused when confronted with the real God of the Bible. A God who allows pain, suffering, disease, murder, and rape.

As an example, let's look at the biblical story of Noah's Ark. The account of Noah's Ark in the Bible is presumably the most popular story Christian parents share with their children. But, why? Because it's a fun story, right? But, why is this account such a *fun* story to tell?

When you truly think about it, at the occurrence of this event, the only person who thought this was a bright and colorful story was....NOBODY! This event, found in the book of Genesis (Chapters 6 through 9) was not fun for anyone on the planet at that time. According to the Bible, we discover that the entire human race of the earth, save Noah and his family, were drowned by God. I'm not sure about you, but being drowned by God is nowhere on my bucket list!

Surely this great flood experience was pleasant for Noah and his family, right? Probably not. Strap your feet in Noah's sandals for a moment, and imagine with me. You are willingly being locked in a huge, dark, floating box. The only other people with you are the members of your immediate family. There are more critters than you know what to do with. Animals that could eat you alive. Beasts that you would never think of being around are now your roommates.

Imagine the smells of the animals and their waste. Imagine the sounds of the people, outside the ark, screaming as the reality of death suffocates their minds. They are all being drowned just on the other side of these thick wooden walls. The crying, the screaming, and then the eerie silence from all those dead, floating bodies outside. The smell would soon be too much to take in. It is the silence and smell of death.

You then realize every man, woman, and child outside of your boat is now dead and has been killed by God. As your head fills up with the reality of what is happening, the gut-wrenching feeling of sea

sickness hits you hard. The sickness is due to the massive amount of water being moved violently across the face of the earth. You feel like a rag doll trapped in a cage with wild animals.

Then you think, *Everything I know, everything I cherish from my childhood, everything familiar to me has just been erased by the hand of God.* Your friends, your land, your house, your town, and your means of earning a living are now gone. It's as if God has taken you and your family and placed you on a foreign planet in a galaxy far, far away. Basically, God has just destroyed your world. Now, take the sandals off and come back to me.

Sounds like loads of fun, right? Wrong! Then, why do we tell our children a totally different and often fictitious story of this terrible account? Is it for their protection? If so, then what exactly are we protecting our children from? From the truth about God and His diverse character? Or, do we make it fun with the hope that they can understand it more easily? If these are the reasons, then later in their lives, they will definitely have trouble comprehending a jealous God, compared to the all-happy, grandfather-type God in the sky they have always been taught and shown.

Then God revealed a question within my heart. Was I the only one teaching a wrong account of Noah's Ark? Could other parents also be wrongly teaching this story? To find the answer to this question, I decided to go to my local Christian bookstore to discover for myself. What I found was shocking.

The evidence provided an overwhelming answer to my questions. I had never realized the inaccurate image parents teach their children about Noah's Ark. In just one single Christian bookstore, I found forty-five books on the topic of Noah's Ark and the Great Flood Judgment. Supporting my hunch, all but 5 books were located in the children's section of this small bookstore. All of the covers on the forty-five books were bright, colorful, happy, and would make any child smile. I realized a great truth, right there in that bookstore. This is absolutely not the image God would have portrayed to our children. The account of Noah's Ark was a terrible judgment brought by the wrath of God. How dare we teach a judgment from

God as something of great fun and amusement! We read cute biblical stories like this over and over to our children, but the Bible actually warns about this popular way of parenting. In the Old Testament book of Joshua we find an account of Israel's new leader, teaching the Word of God to the Israelites. This wasn't just any leader. It was Joshua, Moses' predecessor. Listen to what Joshua 8:34-35 teaches,

> *"And afterward he read all the words of the law, the blessings and cursings, according to all that is written in the book of the law. There was not a word of all that Moses commanded, which Joshua read not before all the congregation of Israel, with the women, and the little ones, and the strangers that were conversant among them."*

There are two great truths here which stand out to me as a parent. First, Joshua stood and read all of the words of God. He read the good. He read the bad. He read the ugly. Joshua didn't hold back one single word of God. He was not swayed by his culture, his crowd, nor his own thoughts. Joshua simply shared with these people, both young and old, exactly what God's word teaches. Blessings and cursings.

Second, verse 35 describes the makeup of this crowd. This crowd contained men, women, strangers (people who knew not Israel's God), and *the little ones.* That's right, the little ones stood with their parents and heard Joshua describe God's blessings and God's cursings.

It seems as if teaching the truth about having a proper fear of God is taboo parenting in today's Christianity. However, if parents don't teach their children about fearing God, who will? Not the media, not the culture, and no social apps will teach this truth. Maybe the bigger question is: What does the Bible teach about having a fear of God?

If you were to do a word search of *fear* in the Bible, you would discover many verses which speak about *the fear of God*. Let's look at just a couple which help to give us a proper understanding of how we should teach our children God's Word.

In the book of Psalms, chapter 19, God shares insight about three of His possessions.

*"The law of the Lord is perfect, converting the soul: the testimony of the Lord is sure, making wise the simple. The statutes of the Lord are right, rejoicing the heart: the commandment of the Lord is pure, enlightening the eyes. The fear of the Lord is clean, enduring for ever: the judgments of the Lord are true and righteous altogether."*

In verse 7, God describes His Law as perfect, able to change lives, a narration of God, and can make a simple person wise. In verse 8, God describes His Statutes as right, making hearts happy, very clear, and shining like a bright light on the spiritually dim eyes. Now, notice what possession God describes in the next verse: The Fear of God.

In verse 9, God describes a proper fear of Himself as clean, pure, and 100% OK to teach. The rest of the verse describes the Fear of God as a fear that is able to stand forever, meaning it is always teachable, no matter the culture. Therefore, the fear of the Lord is a practice which should and must be taught. As Proverbs 9:10a teaches, *"The fear of the Lord is the beginning of wisdom."*

Even Christ is recorded twice in Scripture teaching about the importance of a proper fear of God. In Matthew 10:28, Jesus teaches us to fear God above and beyond anything else because God is able to destroy not only our bodies but our very souls.

I want you to honestly answer this question,

"Have you taught your child to fear a God who can destroy a person's entire existence forever, if that God so chooses?"

Be honest. It's not proper to lie and it's doubly improper to lie to an author, especially while holding his book! Good grief! Are you trying to get struck by lightning?!

To be honest, I must confess: my answer was, "No." Gracefully, and a plus for humans, God has promised not to destroy our souls, yet He does still have this unique and powerful ability. I was not teaching this type of fear to my children.

With this new truth, I had to realize, as a parent, that I should stop injecting into the minds of my children this idea of some soft, fluffy, giggling grandfather in the sky. God is not who we want Him to be. God clearly states, "I am the I AM."

What I found interesting were the many accounts in the Word of God about visions of meeting God in Heaven. The Apostle John was taken to Heaven to transcribe all which God would show him of things to come. We call this account the book of Revelation.

When the Apostle John saw Jesus in all His holiness and power, John did something weird to us. He fell down as if dead. What I find odd is that John didn't run up to his old buddy, Jesus and give him a bear hug, lifting Jesus off his feet. In this biblical account, Jesus was an image to be terrified of because of His great power.

So, how do we start changing our teaching styles to reflect this new truth? I mean, am I to walk around the house at night with a flashlight at the base of my chin, whispering "God is coming to destroy you if you don't mind Him! Good night, sleep tight."

While that would be cool parenting fun, I really don't want to turn my children into one of those weird, self-called doomsday prophets. Nor do I want my children to be so terrified of God, they feel as though they are not able to even speak to Him.

So, how's the best way to focus on God's respectable power but at the same time keep it on an understandable level? My mother used to warn me, "I'm about to put the fear of God in you."

Consequently, her warning usually came just before a spanking. While this gave me a healthy dose of fear of Mom, it never brought on a fear of God. Discipline is very important, and we will discuss this topic in a later chapter, but I believe there is more to discipline than just spanking the fear of God into a child. So, let me give you three simple steps. With these steps, you can begin teaching your children how to fear and respect God.

## The Application of Teachable Fear in 3 Steps

### Step One: In order to teach the fear of God, you must first live in that same fear.

Having a proper fear of God doesn't mean I'm afraid to go outside in a lightning storm, or that I hide under my bed when I've fallen into temptation and thus committed a sin. Having a proper fear of God means having a healthy reverence for God. As parents, we can easily get fear and reverence separated in our minds. But to understand the characteristics of God, these two disciplines must work together.

According to a very basic definition, the word *fear* means an unpleasant and often strong emotion caused by anticipation or awareness of danger. Whereas, the word *reverence* means honor or respect which is felt or shown. These are different definitions yet still the same grouping. Let me explain with a real-life illustration.

Growing up in the country, I got to enjoy many Tennessee summers swimming in the creeks of Smith County. Since the closest swimming pool (both private or public) was 30 miles away, the creek became my water park. The only downside to creek swimming is sharing the water with other creatures.

I didn't have to worry about the fish or the beavers. What I watched for were the snakes. As long as I can see the snake's head above the water, I'm OK with sharing the creek. After all, it is a perfect snake's home. But when a snake disappears underwater, all of a sudden, I'm done swimming.

There are several reasons for my actions. First, I have a healthy fear of snakes. I'm all right with snakes, as long as I can observe them from a safe distance. Secondly, I have a healthy respect for snakes. I respect their habitat and their ability to bite me and then inject poisonous venom into my bloodstream. Third, I don't make up fictitious stories to my children about snakes. I want them to have a healthy fear and respect, just like I have, for all venomous snakes. So, the best way to teach my children the proper way to fear and respect snakes is to show them how *I* fear and respect snakes.

Imagine the horror of teaching your children that poisonous snakes are not harmful and don't need to be respected. Then you brought a box of rattlesnakes into your home and allowed your children to play with them. As a side note: There's not a snake in his right mind that would set scale in my house with all my curious children. Talk about an early shedding of skin!

The point is, if we show our children how to fear and respect something as common as snakes, then shouldn't we show them the same before the One True God?

## Step Two: Don't act like you know everything about God.

One of the reasons why I fear God is that I don't always understand why He does and allows certain things. God is a great mystery to me. There are some things God will do which we may never understand. This should make us fear Him even more.

As if they know every characteristic of God, many parents try to form an image or idea of God to their children. Essentially, we are creating a false god. A god which we can easily understand. A god which needs not to be feared or revered. A god whom we have no trouble explaining to our children. The truth is, we will never fully understand the thoughts or actions of God. Therefore, we should not act like we know it all.

Children can ask some of the deepest questions. Once, my daughter, Jada, asked, "Dad, why did God let Nana get cancer?"

After processing the question and thinking of the best possible answer, all I could say was, "I don't know. I've asked God that same question."

While my answer was given with the best honesty possible, I could have easily responded in a different way. In a parenting way.

Some of my parenting answers could have been: "Jada, God just wanted to test how much Nana loves Him. Remember Job in the Bible? Well, Nana is a modern-day Job." Or "Honey, God had nothing to do with this cancer. It was from Satan!" or "My dearest daughter, thou knowest our God is a god of trinitarianism, consisting of mercy, grace, and cancer."

These answers are parenting answers, but you know what Jada needed to hear? The truth. And the truth is, Daddy doesn't know. We are all just humans, and God is the One Holy God of our universe.

I didn't answer my daughter's question as a fa-

38

ther. I answered it as a fellow Believer. Because of my honest answer to her hard question, she now knows that Daddy doesn't have God all figured out.

After I gave my answer, her facial expression still held that innocent and childish puzzlement as she continued to seek the mystery of God and His ways. One of the best spiritual teachings from you is not to act like you know everything about our God.

**Step Three: Don't sugarcoat the Word of God.**

We will discuss, with more detail, this topic in the next chapter but this step does apply to fearing God. As we've looked at the terrible account of Noah's ark we have to ask, "What other biblical teachings have we sugarcoated for our children?" If you study on it, you may find too many to count. It's high time that a new generation of parents give their children the honest and accurate Word of God.

I believe the reason we tame the Scriptures is to protect our children from fearing God. Odd, I'll admit, but absolutely true. God commands us to fear Him, yet we take those same words and cook them into something sweet and edible for our children.

The prophets spoke some hard words. Jesus often taught in a direct and pointed way. For us to sugarcoat these messages to our children sweeps the fear and reverence, like cobwebs in a corner, from their minds.

So, remember to scare the absolute Noah right out of your child by practicing these three steps. We must not only teach fear but show it! We must not act like we know all about God! And as tempting as it is, we must not water-down nor sugarcoat God's Word to our children! With this mindset we can now begin a process. But it's not a process you may be thinking of.

In the next chapter, I will share with you a truth that, at first, reads as bizarre. It could almost come

across as anti-religious. I want to share with you the
dangers in teaching your children about your religion

# Chapter Recap

**DO:**

• Teach your child, by example, how to show reverence to God and the things of God.

    - Reverence in His house of worship.
    - Reverence for His Holy Word.
    - Reverence for His faithful servants.
    - Reverence in their worship.

• Teach your child the truth through God's Word about the power, might, and vengeance of the Lord. They can handle it.

**DO NOT:**

• Allow your child to be disrespectful in the place of worship.
• Allow your child to mock or degrade the things or people of God.
• Try to give a logical answer to the workings of God, in which you have no clue about.

# CHAPTER 4
# Great in Their Spiritual Relationship

## "Don't Teach Them Your Religion."

I have to tell you. You're doing great. I mean, you have really been persistent in the reading of this book. I'm very proud of you! Go ahead and give yourself a smile or a week's vacation. Just tell the boss I gave you permission, but be sure to take this book with you.

Now, if you're not being persistent in reading this book and it's been like 3 months since you started this book, then what's your problem? Is it me? Is it your time management? Is it laziness? Come on. Get with it. Be consistent. Finish what you started. No vacation for you. As a matter of fact, I want you to stand up and read this entire chapter out loud. That should teach you a lesson...I'm not sure what lesson that is, but I bet it's a good one. Now, back to this chapter.

There are many things I love about my wife, but one of the things I love the most is her memory. I'll admit it's a double-edged sword. Sometimes her memory jousts against mine when it comes to important things like who finished off the ice cream on the night of August 5th, 2006. I know it was her; I just know it.

For the most part, her memory is a blessing. If there is anything I can't find in our house, I turn to her elephant-type brain. She remembers those little things, which I discard. Maybe, it's because I need the room in my mind for other important things like...like...

Regardless, I know whom to turn to when I need help with locating items I've misplaced. This is important because we all have those people whom we depend on to help guide us in different ways. So, when I was twelve years old and had questions about God's existence, I went on a quest to find the person who knew the most about God. As a young boy, this search was easy for me. It had to be my pastor. He was the only man I knew who prayed to this God. I was certain he was the man to talk with.

Luckily, we lived within a quarter mile from the church. So one summer day I snuck out of our front yard, cut through a large field, and soon stood knocking on the back door of the church. The preacher's car was nowhere to be found. Just like a typical preacher.

Eventually, I gave up knocking and thought it best to return home before my mother suspected I had ran away. I definitely didn't want her to give my room away to my little brothers. But before leaving, I curiously twisted on the knob of the church door and to my surprise, the door opened. As a twelve-year-old boy, I felt it was my duty to never pass up a chance for exploration.

Have you ever been alone in a church sanctuary? It's kind of spooky. As a thirty-seven-year-old pastor, I still get a little creeped out when I'm in the sanctuary all by myself at night. There is something sacred and spiritual about a sanctuary when it's silent and empty.

As I peeked around the corner into the sanctuary, my eyes were instantly drawn to the center stage. There was the pulpit. It looked massive and intimidating but different. The only lighting was from the stained glass, narrow windows, perfectly lined along both sides of the room. The sanctuary had two sections of pew seating and a narrow center isle covered with well-traveled carpet. The colored fabric of each pew seemed to hold a story of it's own. The pews were not dirty but well worn and you couldn't really blame them for their appearance; I'm sure they had withheld many hours of sitting, especially with his preaching.

Even the smell of the sanctuary is a vivid memory. It was a mix of old hymnals, wooden pews, starched fabric, and 20 different slight hints of perfume. Surprisingly, it wasn't a bad smell to me, just unique. It smelt like church. I never had taken the time to notice such details until I found myself standing there alone. Besides the sights and smells, there were also questions. Was I committing a sin by being here without the pastor? Does God know that I'm just looking for help and answers? Is God even real or is He simply made up, like Santa?

My questions became so heavy to carry that I decided to sit down in the last pew of the sanctuary like a true backseat Baptist. Any deacon would have been proud.

There I sat, alone, and with more questions than answers. Then a plan came to mind. I will make God prove Himself to me and here's the plan: I will walk to the front of the sanctuary and then look under every single pew. If I find a five-dollar bill, then I will know that God is real. If God can die and come back to life, then surely placing some money under a pew in order to show a boy His existence wouldn't be so hard, right?

I started my search. I diligently and slowly looked under every single pew, giving God adequate time to produce a heavenly bill. I searched until I found myself at the back of the sanctuary where my plan first began. I stood just as broke as when I had arrived. I had gotten my answer. I walked outside, shut the door behind me, and pointed my feet toward the field, which led back home.

The walk back would grant adequate time for hunting. Arrowhead hunting. One of the most valuable treasures a boy could ever hope to discover was an unbroken, authentic, American Indian arrowhead. Farmers would usually plow them up while turning the ground in the springtime. And with it being summer, now was the perfect time to hunt, especially in this field.

Now, there are three basic tools to hunting arrowheads. In case you ever want to hunt for your own arrowheads, here are the tools you'll need.

First, you will need a good stick. This will help for poking at the dirt and turning over rocks so that you don't have to bend over every time you want to inspect something.

Second, you need to know what colors to look for in the dirt. Arrowheads were made out of flint and obsidian rocks. These rocks have a certain color. If you know what you're looking for, you can spot one pretty easily.

Third, you need to say a prayer because arrowheads are few and far between. But, since God didn't provide me with any monetary evidence of His existence, I skipped this step and began my search.

I was almost to the end of the field when I saw it. No, it was not a five-dollar bill tucked under an arrowhead, although that would have been super-cool. Instead, I saw the biggest anthill I'd ever seen in my twelve-year-old life. I had to check it out. It was my duty.

As I got closer to this anthill, I noticed all the ants. They were busy working, moving, following, building, and gathering. I just stood for a minute and watched them work. They didn't seem to be bothered by me at all as I stood looking down over them.

I knew I had the power with one stomp of my foot

to squash them all, but I didn't. Then a thought crossed my mind. What if I wanted these ants to know I was real, how would I show myself? Would I make my existence known on their terms or on mine?

This is when the reality of my foolishness toward God finally sank into my skull. There by that anthill I fell to both knees and apologized to God. If God were going to prove His existence to me, it would be on His terms and not mine. Not long after this experience, God did just that during a Sunday morning service, and I became aware of His existence and my dependency.

The truth I learned so many years ago was carried on into my parenting skills. Just like me, when my children become curious about God and His existence, I know they will actively seek the truth for themselves. However, this is an area where many Christian parents can do more damage than good.

I would like to show you four reasons why we should allow our children to actively search out God for themselves.

### Reason #1: Jesus can swim on His own.

Guess what? We didn't teach Jesus how to swim. Quite factually, he didn't have a need to swim. I once asked a Sunday school class of four-year-olds why Jesus walked on the water. One boy replied, "Because Jesus didn't know how to swim."

The Gospel of Jesus Christ can float on its very own without you or me holding it up. Now, I write this as a preacher. So, you may be asking, "Then why preach?"

Unlike humans, the Bible is absolute truth and absolutely from God. Only the Holy Spirit convicts the souls and only Jesus saves the sinners. We have no right nor authority to perform the miracle of salvation on others. If our children are to accept Christ as their

Savior, it must be in the same manner as I was saved: by the power and grace of God.

While we can shape and mold our children's understanding about who God is and what God expects, there still must come a time in a child's life when he or she actively searches for the genuine truth about God. Therefore, we can teach them about Jesus, but we should be very careful about force-feeding them the Gospel.

As a pastor, I worry about evangelical events which are focused on persuading children to "give their hearts" to Jesus. A good example of this is at Vacation Bible School.

VBS events are packed full of games, snacks, theme nights, bible stories, and friendships. But then something odd starts happening to the preacher as VBS comes to an end. His face starts to turn a deep shade of serious. Then he pulls out his Bible, starts pacing the stage, and begins to preach about how easy it is to become a Christian.

Here is a common result: Some children will come down, repeat a prayer, go home, and never question what just happened. But, as they begin to grow into adulthood something happens.

For the first time in their lives they will become curious about who God really is and what God really expects. For some this will come in the teenage years. For others, this may come later in their adult life. Regardless, they will one day become curious about God and their own salvation.

When we push our children to accept Jesus at an early age, we have not allowed them to use their own curiosity to seek Christ. For some reason, parents have become afraid of a misconception. We feel that if Jesus falls in the water of our children's minds, He might drown and our children will never desire to be saved. This view takes all the authority and power away from the Gospel.

## Reason #2: Jesus doesn't want to play dress up with you.

As a father, I have attended several tea parties, four nail polish competitions, six ballet recitals, and many dress up events, all from the comfort of my living room floor. To my children, one of the funniest things to do is to dress up Dad. They like to polish, powder, prime, and paint me.

Now, I don't mind them using me as a guinea pig, but I would never leave the house that way. I'm all for women wearing makeup, and I believe some women need all the help they can get, but I would never wear makeup intentionally.

As I was standing at the mirror washing my face off from a "let's paint daddy" session, I thought to myself about how Christians do the same to Jesus. Every Christian has a mental image of what Jesus looks like. But, where did we get this image? My guess? Our culture. As a test, let me ask you six basic questions about Jesus, during his earthly ministry. Write your honest answers beside each question.

1. Did Jesus have a short and neatly groomed beard?

2. Did Jesus wear a beautiful flowing robe with a large sash thrown over his shoulder?

3. Did Jesus have long, wavy, blondish hair and blue eyes?

4. Did Jesus have a perfectly shaped American male figure?

5. Did Jesus always show love and never anger?

6. Did Jesus never get hungry or thirsty?

If you answered, "yes" to any of these questions, then you failed the test and you have an unbiblical view of what Jesus looked like and how He acted while here on earth. Jesus was hard to pick out from a crowd of men. He came in the form of an ordinary man, yet he was able to do the extraordinary. Once, he barricaded the doors to a church, made a whip, flipped over tables, and ran the peddlers out the back door. Sometimes Jesus got angry.

The trimmed beard, rosy cheeks, and long, flowing hair? All false. The New Testament has a lot to teach about who Jesus was and how He appeared. There are several examples, but I'll only share one. It's the account of Judas Iscariot giving the "Jesus mob" a sign, which would reveal Jesus from all the other men at the Garden of Gethsemane. If Jesus always appeared in immaculate, glowing, photo-shopped condition, Judas could have simply said, "Just grab the guy who looks like an American hipster!"

So, if we didn't get this view of Jesus from the Bible, then where? You can probably guess, years of culture. Cultures from our past, even in our current, form our images of how Jesus dressed and groomed. Yet, we have no biblical proof that Jesus appeared any different than the rest of His neighbors and friends. In the afterlife, we may stand in the presence of Jesus, asking Him why He cut His hair and why He has a dark tan.

If we understand that Jesus didn't look like we see Him portrayed in most paintings and drawings, then why would we pass this false view of Jesus on to our children? Our children need to form their own biblical view of who Jesus was as a person, who He is as God, what He looks like now, and what the Bible records of His appearance as a man.

So, stop it. Jesus can dress Himself.

**Reason #3: Jesus wants your parental rights.**

I hold many titles at my house. I am the official kitchen cabinet door closer, the toilet flusher, the Magic Eraser King, and, when on the phone, the loudest finger snapper around. Maybe you hold some of these titles in your house as well.

One of the most important titles I carry at my house is the title of Dad. According to the Bible, it's my responsibility to teach my children who God is and what God requires of them (for more on this topic, study Deuteronomy, Chapter 6). Yet sometimes, I find myself wanting to teach my children so many things about church order and the Baptist denomination's way. The problem is, many of these things have nothing to do with Jesus! Are you tracking?

Parents can easily get into a bad habit of teaching children more about the religion of the parents than about the God of the parents. They totally miss the main thing: Teaching children to properly love and serve their heavenly father. Jesus must be taught in a way which allows Him to be the authority in people's lives.

As a pastor, I don't want people to praise me over praising Jesus. As a parent, I don't want my children obeying me over obeying Jesus. Therefore, it's my Christian duty to teach my children that Jesus wants to be the Master of their lives. However, they will never learn this if I never release my children to serve and love Jesus on their own.

So, stop having total parental control. Give it to Jesus.

## Reason #4: True Service will never happen without True Conversion.

Before the Lord called me to preach, I was an over-the-road truck driver. I remember taking my oldest son, Brice, who was around the age of eight at the time, on a short trip in the truck with me. It was his first time out, and we had a blast.

Since an early age, his favorite NFL team has been the Pittsburgh Steelers. This trip brought us close enough to Pennsylvania to get an authentic terrible towel. I gladly bought it for him, finished my route, and steered the truck towards home.

About two weeks later I found the terrible towel caked in mud, ripped, and laying outside in the backyard. I asked my wife if this was an accident, but she admitted that he never took care of this towel. Now, if you are familiar with the terrible towels then you know this is not the way to treat them. It's a show of Pittsburgh pride just to own one. At that moment I was glad we lived in Tennessee and not Pittsburgh. I could have gotten beat down for allowing this to happen in my backyard!

About a year after this event, Brice wanted to take another trip with me. As God would have it, we stuck close to the same route as our previous trip. However, on this trip I made my son help unload my trailer. After some hardball negotiations and promise of a candy bar, I agreed to pay him five dollars-an-hour. And so, we set off with him calculating his future earnings and me enjoying my hard-earned candy bar.

On the route back home, we had a chance to stop at the same place we purchased his first terrible towel. There, neatly folded on a rack, laid a stack of bright yellow terrible towels. To my surprise Brice picked one up, walked to the counter, pulled out his freshly earned money, and purchased a new terrible towel. To this day, some five years later, that towel, in perfect condition, is proudly hanging on his wall.

What would cause Brice to treat two identical towels in two drastically opposite ways? My guess is that Brice was given the first towel, but he earned the second. He understood that the second towel came at his expense. With the second towel, Brice had a true conversion in his mind, which caused his service to the towel to be great.

While we can do nothing to earn God's salvation, there must be a true conversion in order to have a genuine service to the Lord. For this reason, I never ask our children to serve in any way until they have had a heart conversion.

I don't want my children to serve a church or a religion. I want my children to serve the Lord because they have a changed heart. If we gauge our children's spiritual level based on how much they serve the church or their religion, then one day you may find that they have thrown that church or religion in the backyard. And there it will lay on the ground of their hearts, ripped and caked with mud.

These are just four reasons as to why we should not teach our children our own religion. Instead, let's teach our children how to love and serve *their* Jesus.

# Chapter Recap

**DO:**

- Teach your child to always question, with the help of Scripture, other people's views of God.
- Allow your child to search out answers to their questions of who God is and what He requires.
- Realize that the Gospel of Jesus Christ is the only power God will use to grip a child's heart.

**DO NOT:**

- Allow your child to dress up Jesus, according to their own thoughts or ideas without biblical support.
- Teach your child how to serve the church or your religion.
- Allow your child to hunt for arrowheads in the street.
- Desecrate a Terrible Towel.

# CHAPTER 5
## Great in Their <u>Words</u>

### "Practice What You Tweet"

It would be great if every adult actually lived by the truths they often tweet or post on social media sites. Wouldn't that be a great world? There seems to be much more truth in our words which are written than the words which we speak. Why is this? Do words not have the same meaning if they are only spoken? Maybe we should allow my close friend to do the writing for me in this chapter. You probably know him well. His name is Mr. Conviction and he has something to say to us all about practicing what we tweet.

Mr. Conviction always hits me hard. He never softly eases into my mind, but instead he runs up from behind, like a schoolyard bully and gives me a huge, spiritual wedgie. It always feels that Conviction smashes my heart into a billion pieces. Maybe he does the same to you? Let me share an instance where the hammer of Conviction fell and shattered my engorged hubris.

My children have many talents. Let me give you the top five talents they display.

1. They can flood a commode in less time than it takes to tie a shoe.

2. They can individually devour an entire bag of potato chips without anyone's approval or knowledge.

3. They can hide my tools in the backyard so well that only my lawnmower can find them.

4. They can take a shower and somehow come out of the bathroom completely dry.

5. They can ask questions upon questions upon questions.

Maybe your children have some of the same talents, but it's this last talent I want us to focus on in this chapter. The way I responded to this last talent would eventually bring true conviction to my heart and a humble correction in my actions.

The never-ending questions my children would ask caused me to fall into a terrible pattern. Over a period of time, and without my recognition, I had developed several generic responses to my children's questions. I had sharpened my parental skills, in the area of answering questions, down to four common responses. I want us to study these responses individually and understand the dangers each one carries.

### Response #1: "In just a minute."

I honestly cannot tell you how many times I've said this to my children. It was my favorite response and the one I could count on to buy me more time to finish whatever I was doing at the time of the question.

This response was always a lie. It was intended to give me more than a minute. I never once said, "In just a minute," and then looked at my watch, in order to seek the child in exactly sixty seconds. As a parent,

I never saw this response as a lie, but to my children and God, it was.

I remember when I became convicted of this style of lies. It was a beautiful summer evening. We had just finished dinner, and I retired to my desk in my bedroom and began pecking away on a keyboard. I remember my daughters came running into the bedroom with excitement in their eyes and a smile on their face. Then the question, "Daddy, will you come outside and watch our new dance routine?"

It was sweet to see them so excited and energetic about being active. I smiled back at them, gave them both a high-five, and delivered my famous parenting response, "In just a minute."

With shoulders lowered, they left to go back outside. As I spun around in my chair to start back to typing, the Spirit of God gripped my heart, and a thought entered into my mind. One day those girls will not be in my backyard ever again. One day those girls will never dance together again. One day I will be the last person those girls will want to run to.

As I thought about these truths, the Spirit of God spoke once more. "One day all these things will be true, but not this day." I got up from my chair with tears forming in my eyes and walked out on onto our back deck. To my surprise the girls were not dancing. Instead they were sitting on the bottom step of our deck.

Evidently they didn't know I was behind them, and I heard the younger daughter ask her older sister, "How long is just a minute?"

"Well, it depends. Dad's minutes are long, but normal minutes are short."

And there you have it. The hammer of Conviction fell on my heart and shattered me right there on the back deck and left me with a huge, spiritual wedgie. Embarrassing.

I promised God I would never use such lies again to my children. After calling an emergency family meeting that night, I asked my family to hold me accountable to never again respond with this type of lie. Let's just say, I was the one who learned a new dance that day!

Now, when requests for my time come and I need more minutes to finish a project, I will stop whatever I'm doing, look at my watch, and give that person an exact time to talk with them. Sometimes, I will even set a quick reminder on my cell phone so that I don't forget. I vowed to no longer lie about my "just a minutes." Could it be that you too have fallen into this type of response? If so, apologize to all involved, and be more factual when responding to your child. As I started to think about this type of lying, I discovered I had been speaking lies to my children, in more ways than one.

### Response #2: "We'll see. Maybe."

I found myself using Response #1 to buy me more time to continue doing whatever I was doing. However, I would use Response #2 for the times when I just didn't have the heart to say, "No".

The problem with this response is that your child will leave the conversation with just as many questions as before they began speaking with you. I couldn't understand how frustrating this response was to a child until I put myself in the child's shoes. Here, you try them on.

Imagine you have a twenty-five-year-old daughter who told you last night that she is getting married, but here's the catch. The wedding is only 3 months away! The next morning, you reach your boss's office, knock on the opened door, and wait for his attention. He warmly invites you in, and you sit down in the closest chair with an exciting bounce. Your boss has no trouble determining that you have something new to share. He smiles, and you step right into your story.

You know this boss as a good and trusted friend. He's a man you have worked with and for since your daughter was born. And now, after you share your news, he begins to smile just as much as you. He is proud of your daughter and proud of you, as a parent.

As the conversation comes to a close, you officially need to ask your boss for 3 days off of work just prior to the wedding. Your boss smiles again, slightly tilts his head, and tells you, "We'll see."

You know him as a jokester, but you need him to give more of a response than this. I mean, this is the overall purpose of you sharing this news with him. Maybe you misunderstood him, so you ask, "Excuse me?"

"I said, 'We'll see." He quickly spits out.

You leave his office confused and even a little angry.

The next week, after encouragement from your spouse you ask your boss again for those same three days off. His response? "Maybe"

Fast forward to a week before the wedding. Everything is purchased, prepared, polished, and painted. The wedding is coming up fast, and the bride is starting to have the wedding jitters. Your daughter needs you.

At the end of the workday you confront your boss one last time. With a smile, he replies, "We'll see."

Now, you can let your mind take this story on further, but the point has been proven. Getting a response like that is just rude and uncaring. Yet, we so often respond to our children with the exact same words. But a wedding is more important than a broken wheel on a toy, right? Not to the child holding that broken toy.

Remember my reasoning for using this response? I didn't want to tell my children, "No."

So, I would give them the "We'll see" answer in hopes that they would eventually forget about their request all together.

Somehow, this culture has taught parents that it's wrong to tell children "No." Therefore, we constantly

come up with ways to divert our children's attentions when they ask questions that should require "No" as an answer.

I realized that essentially, I was lying to my children by giving them this response of "We'll see." when I already knew the answer.

Today, when I'm faced with the temptation to say "We'll see" or "Maybe", I force myself to make a decision and to give an adequate answer. My children love the fact that they can finally get a direct answer out of Dad.

### Response #3: "Go ask your mother/father."

I wonder how many times parents across the globe, have used this phrase before? I wonder how many different languages this response has been spoken in?

Just like the other two responses, this one has a deeper meaning also, which can cause strife between parents and their children and even between spouses.

I used this response to totally dodge the question that was being asked of me. By far, this was the easiest response to give to any of my children.

Want to spend the night with a friend? Go ask your mother. Want to stay up late on a school night? Go ask your mother. Want to go outside and play? Go ask your mother.

As long as it didn't involve the child's safety or our money, I would always default back to my wife's final decision. And I actually thought that I was doing my wife a favor by "letting her in" on the decision making in the house. There is a Greek word often used for this type of mentality. It's called bologna.

What I was actually doing was causing more stress on my wife and an extra hoop for my children to jump through. All just to save me from having to stop, think, make a decision, and then stand by it.

Even at church, children can be sneaky. One Sunday morning after the service, my son Brice and one of his friends quickly approached me and asked the well-rehearsed question, "Can I go to Kylan's house?"

"I don't care, but go ask your mother." was my reply.

On the way home, and without Brice, my wife asked, "Why did you tell Brice to come and ask me about spending the day with Kylan if you already said he could?" She had a point, as most women do.

My wife was aware that I was simply making it difficult for her and our children by not making a stand-alone decision. It was not that my wife didn't care where our children went on Sundays but rather, my actions showed this was true about me.

The danger of this response is that children will eventually grow up to be young teenagers. These creatures change very rapidly. They begin to smell different. They lose most of their rationality. And they always become aware that the response "Go ask your mother/father" is a parenting cop-out, and they learn to imitate the same behavior.

If we want our children to grow into adults who do great things for God, then we must teach them to make decisions all on their own. I was failing at this. Don't you fail.

Today, I handle these situations totally different. When asked from my child to make a decision, I respond with a "Yes", "No", or "I will need to talk to your mother about this." Did you notice who is talking to Mom about the request? Me, and not the child. I now take responsibility of personally bringing the issue to my wife or making the decision myself.

Because of this new practice, three things have improved in my life.

1. My relationship with my children is better. They can now bring their requests to me knowing that they will receive a decision.

2. My relationship with my wife is better. Now, she and I talk more about our children's requests. We have a better style of communication, and she has more confidence in my decision-making.

3. My ability to make decisions is better. Responding with a decision has made me a better choice maker both at home and at work.

## Response #4: "That's not important."

I didn't use this response as often as the other three but it was one that caused just as much damage. Often my children would come to me with questions, which I knew required an answer that I thought was too difficult for them to understand. As a diversion, I would simply respond, "That's not important, Sweetheart. You're too young to worry about such things."

What I failed to realize is that my children really wanted to know the answers to their hard questions. Children don't ask questions just to shoot the breeze. They really want to know the answers to some difficult questions. Adults have become so trained in the art of asking questions just to keep from having silence, that we sometimes don't care about the answer to our questions.

My wife, Valerie, has often accused me of asking her questions but not caring or listening for the answer. While I'm still doing research on the Internet to prove this theory wrong, I must admit that adults (especially men) do this often. We will ask questions just to break the silence but, in turn, not care anything about the answer.

When it comes to most children, they really want to know the answers to the questions they are asking. Even the difficult ones.

As a prime example, all parents will dodge this question at some point in their lives: "Mommy/Daddy, where do babies come from?"

Now, this is not a shooting-the-breeze question. When kids ask this question, they really want to know the answer. My response was simple, "Honey, that's not important now. One day you will understand." Cop-out.

Here is what I failed to see: My child made a decision to come and ask me this question. They chose to ask me instead of their friends, their teachers, or their grandparents. They came to me for an answer. If I blow them off and decide to dodge the question, I have taught my children that their question was not important enough to me for an adequate answer.

After becoming convicted of my responses in one of my prayer times with God, I committed to start honestly answering all questions. Later that night, as God would have it, my five-year-old son, Camden, asked the dreaded question, "Daddy, how are babies made?" This proves to me that God does indeed have a great sense of humor.

"Sit down, Son, and let me tell you all about it." I said with a smile. Immediately, the room cleared out and after the dust settled, the only people left to converse were Camden and I. So, I began.

I tried to use the proper medical terms for all parts of the reproductive organs and explained what they were used for and how babies are made. To my surprise, I learned more than he did that night. Let me share with you 4 things I learned by honestly answering his question.

1. It gave me a chance to share with my son a biblical view of sex and God's design and purpose for a man and woman. I first learned about sex from a conversation with a friend on the school bus, and boy, was I confused for a long time.

2. It allowed my son to hear reasoning and planning behind why he is shaped a certain way.

3. It showed my son a trust and confidence in getting an answer from his father. And now that the harder questions are over with, it's all downhill from here.

4. It satisfied his curiosity. After answering his question in detail, my son got up from his chair, patted me on the knee, and said, "Thank you, Daddy." And with that, he ran into the playroom and joined in on an aggressive wrestling match with his brothers. I have learned not to use the response "that's not important" and I have been blessed by the change.

But have you ever asked yourself, "Why do children ask so many questions in the first place?"

I think the answer is simple. Children are looking for a satisfying answer. And they will keep asking questions upon questions until they find a satisfying end.

Parents often view this as a bad thing, but it's actually a blessing which can lead to great conversations about God. While all roads do not lead to Heaven, I think all questions do lead to God. Let me give you an example.

Let's pretend that I send my four-year-old son, Abram, over to your house. Don't worry, I always pack them a backpack full of duct tape and carpet cleaner to offset the destruction.

Let's say, I give him these simple instructions: "Go ask _____ a question." (Fill your name on the blank. Go ahead, I know you want to. Actually write your name on this blank. Then, if you ever loan the book out, it will really mess with the reader and they will wrestle with the temptation of wanting to mark through your name and write in their own.)

Here's the question I want my son to ask you: "Where did you get your watch?"

You and I know this is a loaded question. A question, when opened, reveals only more questions.
Abram: Where did you get your watch?

You: From the store.

Abram: Where did the store get the watch?

You: From the people who made the watch.

Abram: Where did they get the watch?

You: They made the watch from different metals and such.

Abram: Where did they get the metals?

You: They got the metals from the ground.

Abram: Where did the ground get the metals?

You: Well, I guess from God.

While my son asked many questions, there was also an underlying theme to all these questions. Did you pick up on it? He basically wanted to know where all things originated. As a child, this question of origin comes in the form of many little questions.

If you stopped answering your child's questions, you would never make it to the question of origins, and you will miss a great biblical teaching opportunity.

The Bible is very clear as to how Christians should respond to questions. In the book of James, chapter 5, the Apostle charges all Christians to be truthful in our answers and promises to others. In verse 12, James tells us there is one thing to remember above all the previous writings of his. It is to let your "yes" be "yes" and your "no" be "no". This sounds simple but is a hard find in our culture today.

James then alludes to the danger in giving false responses. You will become a hypocrite to Christianity and to your children. We can't raise great children for God if all they hear from us are uncaring responses.

# Chapter Recap

## DO:

- Check the yard for objects before you mow.
- Answer your children truthfully no matter their level of understanding.
- Keep every promise you make to your child.
- Ask them some challenging questions from time to time.
- Stop what you're doing, make eye contact, and listen to their questions.
- Send me a bill for the items my children destroyed while at your house. It's OK. Since I've written this book, I've made a gazillion dollars in profits. Ha!

## DO NOT:

- Give a response only to buy yourself more time.
- Give a response only to dodge a hard question.
- Ever assume your child's questions are not important.
- Ever miss a chance to inject God into the answer.
- Ever agree to a spiritual wedgie. It hurts just as much as a physical one.

# CHAPTER 6
## Great in Their Leadership

### "It's Not a Team Until There's a Coach."

High school. Remember that? Wow. For my generation it was like this: Wake up early enough to tight roll your bugle-boys, which set just above your imitation Eastland brown-leather boots. Tuck in your green silk button-up shirt and give a thumbs up to your Bo Jackson poster as you leave to go outside to await the hour long bus ride to school. Once at school, you must drink two cartons of chocolate milk just to get your mind ready for the day's classes.

I have to say, I learned a lot while sitting within the walls of that old school building. I learned a lot about people, relationships, and equations (which, as a pastor, I have yet to use). I learned how to be a mischief maker and was one of the best bakers of this tasty treat. I learned that a guy can run a lot faster than he thinks by simply having his jock strap laced with Ben-Gay.

I learned a lot about football. I learned there is more to the game than just hitting people as hard as you can. There is a strategy to football in which certain plays must be executed correctly to move the ball down the field. On this team, I learned a lot about brotherhood. We were our own click and we were obnoxiously proud of it. There were large amounts of sweat, tears, and laughter in the weight room.

But one of the most important things I learned during those high school years as a football player was this truth: The Coach never sits in the back of the bus.

There is a great lesson to be learned here and I don't want you to miss it. Our coach was not to proud to sit with us players and crack jokes, but instead the coach was focused. We were traveling to a game to execute the plays he would soon call. See, to our coach, winning the game was not all that was on his mind. His judgment was on the line. His leadership ability would be displayed. His very career would be evaluated. The way our team played the game that night was a clear reflection of who he was as a leader. Win or lose, we played football according to his orders. Therefore, on the ride to each game, our coach was a front-seat-sitting focused man.

As a parent you need this same focus in your life. A focus intent on seeing your child become a greater parent than you are now. I remember someone once asking our Coach why he was always so tense on the rides to the games. He responded, "I want my guys to be better football players than I was." Dad, Mom, that's authentic coaching. That's real leadership. That's a genuine investment in the lives of others. So, I must ask, "What are you expecting from your parenting, your coaching, your leadership, your very life?"

The way your child lives will put your judgment on display. The way your child lives will put your leadership on the line. The way your child lives will even put your very career as a parent out in the open. I want my children to one day be better at parenting than I could ever dream of becoming. They may very well be coaching children of their own one day and they will need to see the best example of a parent that I can possibly provide for them.

So where does it all start? Well, it starts with today's men.

Today's Christian men have started sitting on the backseat of the leadership bus when it comes to raising their children to be great. We can blame this lack of leadership on many things: poor examples in Dad's parents, the lack of godly men in the community, the women's lib movement, fear of failure, etc. But placing blame on an event or situation does not help to change your parenting skills today. Blame is not an avenue for improvement nor can blame be used as an excuse to stop from trying new ways to parent. Because of blame, many men have stepped back and left the parenting up to their spouses.

Mom is now seen sitting alone at the front of the bus. She is busy reviewing each child's progress, looking for ways to improve both herself and her children. She is busy working out schedules and finding balance in her parenting. She worries about what the children eat, how they interact with others, where they spend the night, and how well they are progressing in school.

Where's Dad? He's at the back of the bus thumb wrestling with the boys and talking about the latest video game. Dad has become the Weekend Party Planner for the kids, leaving Mom to be the Weekday Leader. While there's nothing wrong with Mom being a leader and Dad having fun with the kids, there is often a great unbalance in our parental roles.

We dads will try to excuse our lack of leadership by saying things like: "Take it easy, Honey. They are only having a little fun. Boys will be boys."

"You don't have to be so restrictive with the kids."

"What's the big deal, Dear? I don't see anything wrong with that?"

"Honey, I have a full time job and you get to spend all

day with the kids. So, naturally you are going to be more of a leader to the kids."

Moms will try to excuse their lack of fun by saying things like: "I can't play right now. I've got to _____."

Is this your situation? Have I just described your family structure? So, how do we move up to the front of our parental bus? Well, as a parent wanting to teach and pass on great parenting skills, you will need to consistently demonstrate to your child four great coaching qualities.

**In your family, show them great <u>Vision</u>.**

I bet you've never been asked these questions: What is the purpose of your family? What is your family's vision? Why are you a family? Are you a family just because some children were produced? What's the big picture or goal for your family?

One of the things I love about my calling as a pastor and writer is the fact that I know my assignments and responsibilities. I know that this week I am responsible for producing, compiling, and passionately delivering three educational and spiritual sermons. I am also responsible for several meetings and I have a writing deadline rapidly approaching. At any given time I can recite to you my responsibilities in both the pastor world and the writer world.

I attend pastoral seminars and writing conferences for the purpose of becoming better at both professions. On the average, I read a book per week to help with my personal growth. I have clear dreams and goals for my professions.

But why is it so difficult to apply this discipline to my family life? Why have you and I not been programmed to think this way? Aren't our families more important than our professions?

When God started my service to the sweet congregants of Laguardo Baptist Church I was scared and unsure of my ability to lead a church to walk closer with the Lord. But something happened within the first couple of months. God gave our church a vision. A set group of goals. A game plan.

God reveled to us a 4 year blueprint of challenges for our church to accomplish for the kingdom of God. This is the greatest and most clear direction from the

Lord that I have ever received. And now that our church is journeying through the 3ʳᵈ year of this 4 year vision, I want to share with you some things I've learned about having a clear vision and purpose for your family. Looking back, I'm glad God gave our church a vision and direction. It helped us to have a purpose besides just conducting church services. And as the leader of the church, it helped me to stay focused and excited about where God has called me to serve.

As a parent, learning these simple truths about a family vision will help you stay focused and excited about seeing your children grow into people of greatness.

**Lesson #1: A Family Vision Should be <u>Selfless</u>.**

The first year of our church vision focused on spiritual and numerical growth of the church. The proceeding three years were a focus on sharing the Gospel and love of Jesus to others in our community, our country, and our circle (global). As a new pastor it was a big pill to swallow, having to rely on God to change people's view on what their church should be. I was so convicted by this vision that during the second year I actually told our people that I didn't care if we added one more member to our flock or not.

Numerical growth was not the focus for that year of service. But guess what? Go on, guess. Nope, I didn't get fired. Guess again. That's right, God didn't grow our church numerically by a little. During that year, God doubled our attendance and membership!

The amazing truth is this: When we took our eyes off of ourselves and our own church, we began to love on others and connect with others in a real way. As a by-product of genuine Godly love and community service, people started showing up at church just to see what all the excitement was about.

A vision or direction for your family must be self-less at its core. This means that I want to see my wife succeed more than I. This means I want to see my children succeed more than I. My family vision should be more about the success of my family and less about the success of me. So, when you think about the plans and dreams for your family, are they plans which only focus on you and your desires? If so, then your family needs a new vision and a new purpose. When searching and planning out your family vision, keep it selfless.

**Lesson #2: A Family Vision Should be <u>Simple</u>.**

There are bible verses that pastors, like myself, love to quote.

*"I can do all things through Christ who*

*strengtens me." - Philippians 4:13*

*" Be ye holy; for I am holy." - 1 Peter 1:16*

*"The prayers of a righteous man availeth much." –*

*James 5:16*

But did you know, there is a bible verse which pastors hate to talk about? It's found in 1 Corinthians 1:27.

*"But God hath chosen the foolish things of the world to confound the wise; and God hath chosen the weak things of the world to confound the things which are mighty."*

I'm pretty sure this is why God called me into the ministry!

I'm foolish and weak enough to be used by God. Now, don't feel too bad for me because you are the one who bought this book which was written by a foolishly weak preacher. When it comes to biblical sense, the simpler equals the better. And when you think about it, this idea works well in many other areas.

The vision God gave our church was a very simple vision. I think it needed to be this way because I'm a simple preacher who preaches a simple message to simple people. Now, when I use the word *simple* I don't mean *dumb*. Instead, it's a feeling of finding great contentment in the simplicity of our lives. Our church vision was as simple as watching a rock hitting the center of a pond. We started our church vision by examining ourselves as a church. Then we rippled out our love and service into our community. From there, God moved us into a focus on our country by making available several mission trips within the States.

Next year will be a focus on international mission work. Here is the beauty of simplicity. After our international focus, the four year vision starts back over with a focus on examining our church once again. Just like our church vision, our family visions need to be just as simple.

I must confess, I struggled for several months trying to acquire a vision or set goals for my family. In my writing, the previous chapters seemed to flow as fast as I could type. But when it came to this portion of my writing, I became stumped. I prayed. I planned. I performed writing exercises. I wrote freelance work. But I was at a writing standstill with *Parenting the Greats* simply because I couldn't come up with a solid vision or plan for my family.

One night after dinner, I called a family meeting. After seven children, anytime my wife or I call a family meeting, all the older children look around at each other and say (almost in unison), in their prophetic voices, "Mom's pregnant." So, after spending some time convincing them otherwise, I began the family meeting with the same question I asked you earlier, "Why are we a family?"

My older children are used to my style of preaching in which I often ask rhetorical questions to the congregation. So, they were waiting for me to answer my own question. What shocked them was when I told them that I really needed to know the answer to this question because I did not have an answer. Only then did the mental gears star turning in their minds.

After several minutes of conversation the answers to my question were surprisingly simple. Maybe all this time I had been over thinking and complicating a simple vision for our family. From our children, the overall responses revolved around love. Because my wife and I fell in love, we now have children whom we love. While this gave reason for our family, it failed to show a vision or future purpose for our family. And then, my wife spoke a sentence which reminded me of the very purpose for this book you are now reading.

"We are a family with a focus on raising up people to do great things for God."

Wow. Somewhere along the way of writing I had lost my focus as the author of this book and as the leader of my home.

This is now our vision and focus as a family: To invest in people and lead them to become great in their own lives. Yes, it's that simple, as it should be. You may be like I was - raising a family without much vision or purpose. I pray you will become serious about finding your own goals and plans for your family. Or you can borrow ours. It's not proprietary!

The church I serve was not started by me. Despite what my children think, I was not around in 1892. But now that I am the leader of this flock, it's my responsibility to lead with a purpose and a vision. You may have lived many years without a family vision or purpose, but that can change today. It's not too late to start showing your family a selfless and simple vision for their future.

### Lesson #3: A Family Vision Should be <u>Sharable</u>.

Since publicly launching our church vision, other churches have also adopted and adapted the same four year plan. Some church leaders have called asking permission to use our vision and others have not. Yet, I feel as if the vision God gave our church is good enough for all churches no matter their size or situation.

This is how your family vision should be - sharable. It's my hope that our children will one day adopt our family vision into their own families when that time comes. A good godly vision should be sharable.

Since the first draft of this book, there have been other families who have taken on our same family vision and have made it their own. This is great news to me as a writer! That's really the whole purpose of why I write - to see others grow closer to each other and to God.

One great thing I've learned about writers and readers - we love to share. We share ideas. We share stories. We share events. We share life. So, make your family vision so selfless, so simple, and so sharable that any child or family could follow along in the footsteps of your vision. Show your family a great vision!

But is this all we need to demonstrate great parenting? No. We can have the best goals and visions designed specifically for our family but if we lack these next three things, you will likely never see your leadership aspirations come true.

## In your family, show great <u>Compassion</u>.

As a Christian, I am to resemble Christ in my living, speaking, praying, and compassion. We all know that God is a God of compassion. But are God's people, people of compassion?

There is a short verse in the Bible which motivates me to be a Believer of compassion. It's Jude 1:22 which reads, "And of some have compassion, making a difference."

Simply put, I am to show compassion to some people because is makes a big difference. And here's the beautiful thing about obeying this verse: It makes a difference in the person's life and in mine.

When I show compassion to the people whom God leads me to, then they are blessed and I am blessed. But God's power doesn't stop there. As I show compassion to others, my children see this.

Now, in a fallen world, compassion always comes with some questions. Why are you helping me? What's in it for you? What's the catch? Not only are the needy asking these questions but also your children are asking the same. If they see you showing compassion with genuine and true motives, they will be changed.

When we decide to show compassion to others, the Bible proves true. It makes a huge difference in the lives of many more people than we can realize.

One of the worst things to see is my children being un-compassionate to a person who I thought they should have helped. Whether it's holding the door for a person in a wheelchair or helping someone who has dropped her groceries in the parking lot, I expect my children to see compassionate opportunities. Maybe you feel the same as a parent. I think all parents should feel this, Christian or not. If this is true, then would it not be true in the relationship of our own salvation?

If God is our Father, through Christ Jesus, then would He not have the same emotions as a parent, when we pass up opportunities to serve others who need our compassion? Since we are adults, we have become quite good at wrapping our non-service in excuses. I'm too busy to stop and help. I'm running late already. I'll mess up my good clothes. I don't have the money to spare.

I hate funerals. Funerals are hard for me. As a pastor, I've had to stand before hurting and heartbroken families. It's hard to see your church family hurting so much and all you can do for them is to give them your words and your prayers. It never seems like that's enough. I wish I could do more to help, but I'm not the Great Comforter.

After the funeral service, there's usually a procession of cars following the hearse. The police will lead, then the hearse, then I'm somewhere following after. We have just left a very sad and emotional service and we are now on our way to place a dead body in the ground and cover it up with dirt.

As I'm driving in the procession I'm always saddened by the looks of the passing drivers as they pull over on the shoulder of the roads. I'm saddened because most of them look angry that a procession has stopped their forward progress. Many of the faces I pass are looking down and growling at their watch. I've even seen some mouth curse words.

Of all the funeral processions I've been a part of, I've never seen one take longer than 2 or 3 minutes to pass by an oncoming car. Why is it so hard for us to take 3 minutes of our day to show love and respect to a hurting family and a deceased human? If it saddens me to see this type of behavior from my fellow countrymen, then I wonder how much it saddens the great Author of compassion.

The truth is I'm a child of God leading my own children towards my God. If I don't take the time to show compassion then neither will my children. Plain and simple.

In your family, show great compassion. And remember, according to God's Word, it will always make a difference.

**In your family, show great <u>Wrath</u>.**

Yep, you read that right. I know some of you parents just got excited and are searching for a big switch to use on your child but let me explain some things first.

In our culture it's hard to talk about the wrath of God. It doesn't compute in our minds because all of our lives we have been taught about the love of God. All of our childhood Sunday School classes were about Jesus loving on others, God showing compassion, and how we should never become angry or upset at others. Most sermons we hear speak about the amazing love of Christ, and boy is it amazing! But is what we have been told all our lives true? I believe it is. The problem is that we were not taught about God's other qualities including His great wrath.

Since God is holy and always true, every characteristic which He displays is perfectly fine for us Christians to show. His grace. His mercy. His love. His forgiveness. These are some of the best qualities we should emulate. The problem we humans run into is picking and choosing which characteristics to display and which to ignore.

By doing a simple word search through the Bible you will discover that the word *wrath* is used almost 200 times. God doesn't hide the fact that He is a wrathful God. Just read for yourself the many times God tells us, through His Word, about His wrath.

We have formed this idea in our common theology that God's wrath is only given to the wicked and disobedient of this world. But this is an unbiblical view of God's great wrath.

In Hebrews 12:4-8, God has some strong words for His children whom the world calls Christians.

> *"Ye have not yet resisted unto blood, striving against sin. And ye have forgotten the exhortation which speaketh unto you as unto children, My son, despise not thou the chastening of the Lord, nor faint when thou art rebuked of him: For whom the Lord loveth he chasteneth, and scourgeth every son whom he receiveth. If ye endure chastening, God dealeth with you as with sons; for what son is he whom the father chasteneth not? But if ye be without chastisement, whereof all are partakers, then are ye bastards, and not sons."*

These verses tell us that the wrath of God is there for our good. To help us in our faith. To grow us as Christians. To teach us discipline and order. If God's wrath is good for his children, then wouldn't a parent's wrath be good for their own children? The problem comes when we parents try to display wrath in the wrong way. So it's important to know the appropriate way to show wrath.

The very biblical definition of the word *wrath* means to show anger. Therefore, parents need to understand what and what not to become angry about. As a rule, I try to only show anger at the things which I understand God to be angry at. Being angry is not a sin. The Bible tells us to be angry, yet sin not. I get angry when I see others mistreated. I get angry when people lie to me. I get angry when others take advantage of me. I get angry when I see people fall into a lifestyle of sin. Not only is it alright to show righteous anger, but it's one of the best characteristics of God. Let me explain.

As a Christian, if I know that God finds anger in

the sin of pornography, then I will be less likely as a child of God to want to partake of this sin. I don't want to anger or displease the very One who I love and serve, the very One who saved my soul and provides for me every breathe I'm blessed to breath. In the same light, this type of relationship should also be true for parents and their children.

My children should see in me a disappointment when they make the wrong choices, when they fall into sins, when they mistreat others, and when they just flat-out disobey.

The word *chasteneth* in the Bible means to discipline in a way that teaches. My anger and disappointment towards my children's bad behaviors should be used to teach and train them in the correct behaviors.

This idea of chastening gives us great liberty in the way we carry out our discipline. What I discovered very quickly in my parenting is that every child of mine responds to types of correction differently. My daughters only need one of my John Wayne squinted-eye looks and they will be squalling at the top of their lungs. At that moment, to my daughters, I am showing great wrath with just a look. My boys, however, require more of a hands-on-bottom approach in order for them to learn from their wrongs.

As our older children have grown into teenagers, the display of a righteous wrath has taught them to love and obey someone much greater than their own parents. It has also taught them all a great truth which is taught in the Bible: Sin will never go unpunished. If this is true, and I'm certain it is, then by me not showing my wrath and letting my children learn from it, I have caused them to accept a lie. The lie being that their sins can continue without any recourse. In your family, show them a great and biblical wrath which will help them to be great parents.

## In your family, show great <u>Love</u>.

A Great Love? What are the differences between an ordinary love and a great love? Tons. An ordinary love is often mingled with other feelings such as the desire of self-gain, lust, and attention. But a great love finds its fluid in none of these desires.

A great love will bring into your life something that you've probably never stopped to think about. A great love brings order to your life. If a great hatred brings a chaos of emotions and disorder to your heart, then wouldn't a great love bring just the opposite? Indeed it does. If you grew up in a home which lacked the demonstration of a great love, then I can pretty much promise you that there was disorder in your childhood. In those memories you will often find pain and chaos.

However, if you grew up with a great love being shown and poured into your life then you would have experienced a beautiful order and a solid structure in your idea of love. In those memories you will often find safety and comfort.

So what type of order does a great love bring? I mean, how can we gage such things?

When you think about it, if you receive or show a great love for someone else, what happens is that you bring an order to the relationship. The relationship no longer has any flavor of unfaithfulness or chance of dysfunction. Because I love my children with a great love, they never have to fear my abandonment. They never have to fear me not loving them with all my heart. They never have to fear that my love will become conditional to their actions or their beliefs.

With a great love for your child, there can be times of discipline and times of correction without the fear of your child hating you or disconnecting from you. There is great safety in a relationship built on a great love for one another. But order in a relationship is not all that a great love brings.

Having a great love in your parenting also allows for order in the area of communication with your child. I have counseled adults who have issues with their parents. When we get down to the heart of the issues, we often discover there is a lack of communication between the parents and child.

If you take a step back, you may discover there is a lack of communication in your family because there is a lack of order. Now, take one more step back and you will see there is not a great love displayed nor demonstrated well in the home. Put that in forward motion and you have this value: No great love = No family order = Pour communication.

I always want to welcome my children's questions, thoughts, dumb ideas, funny jokes, hurting cries, and quiet talks in the car. But they will not allow this type of open communication in our relationship without knowing there is a great love given to them.

Start having a great love for your family today by displaying order and injecting communication into every possible moment. But why is all this so important?

Your child will need to be great in the area of parenting if for no other reason than our rapidly changing culture. Your child may very well face parenting issues which you never dreamed of having to handle.

Just think about the way our culture has changed since you were a child. There are things which I was allowed to freely enjoy as a child which I can not allow my children to enjoy today. There are new dangers, more predators, and greater temptations all looking for ways to destroy the Christian family of today. We need to realize that our children will one day face challenges which will make us say, "I'm glad I'm not raising kids today!"

And remember, it's not a team until there's a

coach. So, be a coach of the best team in the whole
world – your family!

# Chapter Recap

**DO:**

- Remember that you've been called to coach the best team in the world – your family.
- Make a family vision today.
- Show them a great love, compassion, and wrath.

**DO NOT:**

- Hoard your family vision motto. Share it with other families.
- Withhold your righteous wrath. Remember, you can show righteous wrath without physical discipline.
- Restrict the communication in your family. If you do, it will start a negative chain-reaction.

# CHAPTER 7
## Great in Their Devotion

**"How to organize family and personal devotions"**

I suppose Deuteronomy chapter 6 is the spiritual framework of parental responsibilities. By reading the standards God placed in Deut. 6, it's easy to see the high priority God has placed on the parents to biblically train their own children. Yet, many Christians still view the church as the primary spiritual teacher of their children. But when we do this, everyone misses out. The parents miss out on the joys of biblically leading their kids. I love that my children come to me about spiritual matters and questions.

Not only do the parents miss out but the children do as well, by only being taught during church services, which are traditionally held no more than three times each week. Three hours each week to teach your child biblical truths that they will need to be passionate Christians is simply not enough. The church also misses out when we depend on it to train up our children. The church misses out by not having families growing together at home and serving together at church. So, if the home setting is the best place to train up our children, then where do we begin? What family structures can we start at home that help to spiritually grow our children?

I have found that the easiest way to help biblically train my children is through a routine family devotional time. Over the last 20 years family devotions have gotten a bad rap. These devotional times are often seen as a homeschooling, indoctrinating, cultic practice. They are viewed with these identifiers mainly because of the popular myths about family devotional times.

I had bought into some of these myths until I started to try a family devotional for my own family. I must confess, it has been a growing and evolving process during the years. It seems to change as our children grow both spiritually and socially. While there are many myths of family devotionals, I have compiled my top 4 myths/excuses which I used to justify skipping the whole family devotional thing. I hope you will find, as I have, that these are myths and should not be used to keep your family from growing closer to God.

**Myth #1: Family Devotions must resemble a church service.**

When my wife and I first attempted to start a weekly family devotional we had no clue what to do. We found no books on this subject nor did we know of any families doing devotionals who we could ask for advice. As children, my wife and I never grew up with family devotions. So, we turned to the only model of a biblical gathering which we knew - the church service.

Comical now, but serious then. Having five children at that time allowed for ushers, greeters, a music director, a special singer, and me, the pastor. I wish I was making this up, but it's true. And yes, you were expected to tithe but clothing was optional. While this structure for a devotion might work well in other families, it failed miserably with ours. The children treated it just like a church service by coloring in their notebook-papered-bulletins and sleeping on the couch pews.

But, why did this setup fail for us? Reflecting back I can see how our family devotions have progressed into a better experience over the years. Here are some tips that will help your family devotionals be unique.

**Don't be impersonal.** Just like "big church" you are expected to sit still and listen to the preacher talk. This is hard for most adults to do even while surrounded by a crowd of people. Now add in the fact that these are children in the comfort of their own home, and you have a recipe for nap time. Family devotions should always have a personal feel to them.

**Don't be too structured.** Ever notice how the order of a church service is always the same from Sunday to Sunday? While this works well for large crowds, it just didn't work for our family devotions. As soon as we feel that the devotions are becoming repetitive, my wife or I will change the order of our family devotions. We might move our prayer request time to the beginning of the devotional and do our singing at the end. This helps keep our family devotionals from becoming repetitive in its order.

**Myth #2: Family Devotions require a lot of time.**

Family devotionals should not be a full time ministry. It doesn't require hours of preparation, great times of prayer, or wrestling over what to share. There are no committees to be formed nor votes to be lobbied. I structure our family devotionals to be no more than 10 minutes of teaching. The rest of our time is allotted for questions/answers and prayer requests.

So, make your lessons short and don't walk in to your family devotional loaded for bear and ready to bring the hammer down.

**Myth #3: Kids think Family Devotions are boring.**

Parents can often give an excuse of not holding family devotions because their child will see these devotions as boring. However, this myth is far from the truth. I've never had to drag a child or even pre-teen to a family devotion time. In fact, our children often remind us of our family devotional times.

Here are some tactics we've implemented in our family to reassure boring-free devotionals.

1. Select a different person each week to pick the topic for the next devotional. Instead of following a lesson plan or Bible study guide, allow the younger children to pick out the Bible story for the next week's devotional time. They will often pick out the more popular and exciting stories in the Bible such as David and Goliath.

2. Allow your pre-teen and teenager to pick out social topics to discuss for the next week's family devotional. Don't be fooled into thinking that your teenager doesn't have questions about some of today's hottest moral and cultural topics. Even if you home school, your teenager will have moral and social questions which need to be answered. Who better to turn to than you, the parent?

3. With each family devotional, make sure to include a prayer request time. What a wonderful habit to learn as a child - the importance of lifting your friends up in prayer to God. The best way to teach this is to ask for their requests and their burdens and pray with them.

4. Always have a family devotional format which al-

lows for questions and answers. This is always the favorite part of our devotional times, both for the children and for Mom and Dad. We usually have our Q&A time at the end of our lessons, that way all the questions which formed in the children's minds during the lesson can now come out and play in an open field of answers. And if you've ever done a Q&A with your child, then you know that questions always lead to more questions. Before you know it, you've had an hour long bible study with your family and your child has satisfied many of their spiritual questions. Family devotions never have to be boring.

**Myth #4: Family Devotions do little good.**

This is one of the biggest myths there is about family devotionals. Many studies have been done to prove the advantages of family time. In a culture of constant motion and moral decay, sitting and studying God's word together as a family is a true blessing. Your children will always remember the times the entire family studied and discussed together over God's word.

They will remember the answers you gave them to their hard questions. They will know what it's like to lead a family spiritually. They will be proud in the fact of knowing that at least once a week they get to ask you anything they want. They will love the set times of praying together and they will not want to skip a week of devotions. They will accept the responsibility of picking a topic or lesson plan for the upcoming devotional times. Don't ever believe the myth that family devotionals do little good for the child, parent, or family. It's just not true.

## Personal Devotions

This is a tricky task to teach because it must be taught by example and not by words stacked inside a living-room lecture. One of the most bizarre statements I ever read from Christ is found in the Gospel of Luke. In Luke 9:62 Jesus tells us, "No man having put his hand to the plough, and looking back, is fit for the Kingdom of God."

You've got to admit, this is a bizarre teaching. Are we to have a degree in plowing before we can be fit for the Kingdom of God? What exactly is Christ implying by this image of a farmer? How can a person become *fit* enough for the Kingdom?

I think the object of this lesson is this: If you focus on plowing the straightest and deepest spiritual life you can, then your family will have a wide and easy row to walk down and follow. Can you imagine a farmer who's always looking over his shoulder while plowing?

The uneven and shallow rows would not only look bad but would not grow a healthy crop. This is especially true in teaching children about having a personal devotion time.

I've never verbally given a lesson on personal devotions, yet my oldest children have their own because they see Mom and Dad having personal devotions. Therefore, the best way to teach your child how to plow is to plow well yourself. Let me give you 7 tips on devotional plowing.

## 7 Personal Devotion Tips

**1. Have Devotional End Caps.** Each day needs to begin and end with a personal Bible time. In the early morning hours my oldest son, Brice, would always shuffle his waking legs through the house and see me in my chair reading and studying my bible. One morning I noticed him carrying his bible through the house. After about a week, I found him one morning on the couch, sitting quietly, and reading his bible. While more of our little ones are still asleep and miss my example of study, they are well awake in the evening hours. This is where they see me or my wife in our evening studies and they already try to mimic what we do even though they don't understand why we are studying.

**2. Use Assistance If Needed.** If you are not sure how or where to start, there are many resources just for personal bible studies. There are classics and more modern guides that are available but don't completely rely on those sources while leaving your bible unopened. Being a pastor, I use my personal study time to read and study in areas of the Bible which I'm not currently teaching or preaching through. This gives me the freedom to study for myself and not for the purpose of teaching it to others. I can take my time, hang on a phrase for a week, and not be pressured in having to complete my study before a church service.

**3. Don't use a *Read through the Bible in a year* program.** Oftentimes, the only thing most people accomplish after finishing a reading plan like this is bragging rights. Very little of the Bible is retained when reading it in the format which most of these programs offer. Why are we studying the Bible in the fist place? When, as a Christian, am I not going to study the Bible? It's a life-long book which will be held in my hands almost daily for the rest of my life. I want to understand it, not just read through it. Sometimes you may need to hang on a word or a verse for a couple of days, soaking in the meaning of God's rich words.

**4. Always study with a Pen and Pad.** Being a writer, I keep a journal with me pretty much all the time. It helps to know that I have access to write down my thoughts whenever I think of such things. If you start carrying a journal or pad around with you, you will find that it will become quite useful to your life. I have notes, grocery lists, designs not yet patented, cartoon sketches, sermons outlines, prayers, future Facebook posts, book ideas, poems, and several coffee stains all packed within the cover of my journal. I would say that my journal is like a faithful dog by my side, keeping many secrets and smelling better. While I have yet to name my journal, I do plan on keeping it on a shelf for my children's future entertainment when I'm long gone.

**5. Balance your Devotion Time.** I've found that it's good to break my study times up into equal amounts. I set aside time to pray, read Scripture, write thoughts, and just sit and reflect. I do all this in the slowness of the morning and the quiet of night. It's a well guarded treasure of mine mainly because I get so much out those times.

**6. Don't make it into a Marathon.** You're not in a Bible study competition. My bible study times usually last no longer than 30 to 40 minutes each morning and the same in the evening. With my calling, I have the privilege of great amounts of study time during the day and can mix more study time in throughout.

Before being a full time minister, I would use my breaks at lunch to continue in my studies. You would be amazed at the influence you will have at your profession just by people seeing you studying during your free times. It speaks louder than your voice. But don't study your bible and neglect time with your family. Don't study your bible while you need to be working. It's not a marathon. It's a lifestyle.

**7. I added this fake tip** just because I don't like to end a list on the number 6. I know...weird, right? It's not that I see the Mark of the Beast in every 6 I see, but that's just how I'm wired. So, you can add your own tip here.

Along with the family and personal devotions my family loves to play. In closing this chapter, I've decided to share with you some of the games that my family play from time to time. I hope you make as much memories with these games as we have.

## Family fun games that are free

Who says family time has to be boring or expensive? Here are 5 games guaranteed to get the entire family involved.

**Black-Out Night**: Our kids love this one! Once a month we have a "Black-out Night." We prepare for the night by unplugging and turning off all electrical items. When the sun sets we can no longer use any electricity (except for central heat and air). We turn off all appliances, cell phones, laptops, video games, and lights. We cook on the grill. We carry candles whenever we go from room to room. We read books, play board games, and eat dinner all by candlelight and without the humming and ringing of electronics. Basically, we unplug ourselves from the outside world and focus on what's inside the house.

Here is what my wife and I have discovered after several times of doing Black Out Night:

1. Our children stay in the living room with my wife and I. Yes, they are probably fearful of being in their rooms alone in the dark, but it works. We experience great family time.

2. They love being responsible for carrying their own light with them wherever they go (parental supervision of course).

3. When Black-out Night comes, the children literally sit at the window and wait for the sun to set.

4. Storytelling is best told by an open flame.

5. Bed time is a sweet time when you say, "Good night" and then blow their candle out.

Note: Summer months are best due to longer daylight allowing parents with busy schedules to still be a part of this game.

**The Story Game:** Another favorite. On special nights (someone's birthday or another tooth is pulled) we play the Story Game. I will start telling a fictional story. The story will usually be as wild and impossible as I can possibly concoct. After I have started the story, I will not end it but will pass it on to the child next to me by saying the phrase "...and then?" The child next to me will then continue with my story but will put his or her spin on it. When that child is done they will pass on the story with the same phrase "...and then?" This will continue until the last one left to add to the story is Mom. She will end the story, which by now has taken many twists and turns.

Here is what my wife and I have discovered after several times of doing the Story Game:

1. This helps develop our children's imagination, skills in storytelling, and constructing mental atmospheres that are funny, scary, unbelievable, and pretty cool.

2. This is best played just before bedtime. After the

game, the kids get tucked in while still thinking about the overall story that was built by the entire family (well, those that are old enough to speak coherently). You can almost see the story continuing in their eyes as they fall asleep.

3. Talk about funny? Wow. I've never laughed so hard as hearing my children come up with hilarious stories and circumstances.

4. There is something special about hearing my wife make up a fictional story on the spot and making it funny, witty, and a perfect end-cap with each story. It always helps to build up our marital relationship.

**Backwards Night:** Once a month we have a "Backwards Night". Often and especially with a very systematic family, we find ourselves in a predictable and dull routine. On Backwards Night we focus on breaking out of this rut. On this night we perform everything backwards.

During dinnertime, my wife and I will swap seats. The boys will also swap with the girls. You wouldn't think seat swapping would be a big deal to children but it sure is to children with Baptist roots. We will also eat our dessert first (a big favorite).

Clothes will be worn backwards and children's picture-books will be read backwards (from the end of the book to the beginning). We will also challenge the children to tell the entire family simple stories like "The Three Little Pigs" but they must tell it backwards. This is great fun and very hilarious. The kids will even try to walk throughout the house backwards (Do NOT try this on stairs!).

Here is what my wife and I have discovered from Backwards Nights:

1. It's beneficial for our children to experience a dif-

ferent daily routine.

2. Our children performing the storytelling backwards is very challenging and forces thoughts about story building and story order.

3. It's also good for me to step out of my daily routine at home.

4. Eating the dessert first is a winner every time!

**The 5 *Sense* Game**: Place one empty cup or bowl in the middle of the group. Then give each player 5 pennies. One person (the Moderator) will need a blank sheet of paper and a pen to record the answers. Note: The Moderator can participate in the game as well. Here are the questions the Moderator will ask the group:

1. What is your favorite thing to smell? Anyone that wants to share their answer will have to put one of their cents into the cup or bowl. They will then share with the group their answer. The moderator will not move to the next question until everyone has placed a penny in the cup and gives an answer to this question. After everyone has had their turn answering the above question, the moderator will then ask the next question.

2. What is your favorite thing to taste? The group will then repeat the same steps as above.

3. What is your favorite thing to hear? Repeat the same process as above.

4. What is your favorite thing to touch? Repeat the same process as above.

5. What is your favorite thing to see? By the time the Moderator asks this last question every player should have one penny left in his possession. After all questions have been answered, the moderator can start the game over by redistributing the pennies and asking a new set of questions: What is your worst thing to smell, taste, hear, touch, and see?

We played this as a family and we had a blast! We have a three year-old that used the word "snake" as his answer on every single question, which made for many laughs. It was interesting to learn of my wife's favorite things to smell, hear, and touch. It was also a great educational tool for our children in relating how they use their own five senses; they really had to think of practical ways in how they use and experience these senses.

I also took the opportunity at the end of this game to speak to our children about God granting humans the ability to experience His creation in so many different ways. It was a great time of sharing and relating God's purpose for our senses.

I have a desire for my children to grow up understanding and experiencing how fun it is to imagine and build stories on the spot; how fun it is to express yourself through spoken dialogue; and how fun it is to spend a lifetime dreaming and sharing life experiences with others through communication. These simple games are guaranteed to inject a love for personal and appropriate expressions of communication into the heart of your child.

# Chapter Recap

## DO:

- Have Q&A times in every family devotional.
- Plow your spiritual row as straight and deep as you can, so that your family can easily follow.
- Eat you dessert first on Backwards Night. You are welcome.

## DO NOT:

- Rely on the church to Biblically train up your child.
- Be too structured in your family devotional times.
- Ever end a list on the number six... ever!

# CHAPTER 8
## Great in Their Own Skin

### "Stare But Don't Compare"

Most memories of my childhood are great but let me be honest with you, instead of lying to you. Some memories just down right stink. Do you have memories like that?

I have the memory of Greg, my personal 7th grade bully. Not many kids in my childhood days were privileged enough to get their own personal bully, but I guess I was, what Greg would call, "special". I remember Greg throwing me out of my seat and onto the floorboard of the school bus. The bus driver's laughter and my classmates' snickers are still familiar sounds in my mind. Now, twenty-three years later, when I ride a bus I'm always sizing up the passengers. Why? Because I have to buy my own clothes now, and I don't want to mess them up. Eventually, this memory would be overshadowed by memories of self-confidence from the year I outgrew Greg and became stronger, taller, and had much cooler hair.

By now you must be asking, "What does this have to do with this chapter?" The answer is absolutely nothing. But good job on reading it all the way through and not skipping. Now, back to this chapter of staring but not comparing. I do have one more memory I would like to write about. It's a memory of one single comment made by my mother towards me when I was young, probably around the same years of Greg's empiric reign.

In this memory, I was in my room writing one of the most important letters a young child will ever write. I was writing out my Christmas list. Even though Thanksgiving had just ended I was already preparing for the gifts I would unwrap on Christmas morning. My mother walked through my bedroom door and curiously asked, "What are you doing?"

"I'm making my Christmas list!" I energetically answered.

You could tell by the wrinkle above her nose she was weighing her reply.

"Well, Mrs. Sally said her son, Josh, has never once asked for a Christmas gift. And she never has to fuss at him to make his bed or clean his room." She spoke while staring at my unmade bed. She then turned and walked away.

As a parent, I now understand my mother's tactic. Make the boy comprehend there are other things more important in life than Christmas presents. Things like making your bed and being content.

Today, if you were to sit my mother down and interrogate her in hopes of a tearful confession of this diatribe, you would be wasting your time, and you would lose money on the fake mustache you purchased just for this interrogation scene.

It's not that my mother has been trained in counterintelligence drills or is a hard nut to crack, but rather, my mother would not have the faintest memory of her comment made over twenty-three years ago. To her, it was insignificant. It was ordinary. It was a parenting tactic used to move her child toward obedience. Maybe you have used this same tactic on your child just recently.

While my mother's denunciation may have worked for the purpose of causing me to feel guilty and less of a "good boy", it is still very vivid in my memory. As parents, we should try to guard our words very carefully when talking with our children about other boys and girls.

I'm not sure who this Josh boy turned out to be, but I can somehow picture him today, living in a Guinean hut, giving his millions away to a small village, and providing free dental care through his lucrative dental company. And yes, he's probably straightening the sheets on his cot as I type out this sentence. What a good boy! And here I am, writing this book that by now you are sorry you ever purchased. Why do I feel as though this Josh person is superior to me in character even though I've never met the man? Because my mother told me he was.

With the many different hats parents must wear, we often and unintentionally do more harm than good to our children's self esteem when using this tactic. Therefore, it's OK to recognize the good qualities and accomplishments of other children, but not as a tool to use against our own children. Most children are known for comparing themselves to others without the help or suggestion from their parents. The very first brothers we find recorded in the Word of God fell prey to this type of negative comparison.

Cain and Abel were the children of Adam and Eve. They were both hard workers. In Genesis Chapter Four, we find the account of these brothers stepping into the scene. Abel found himself as a keeper of the family sheep; while Cain took on a life as the family farmer. I should note, many preachers portray Cain as a slothful person. The Bible states very clearly that both of these youngsters were hard workers. The problem was not in their work ethic but rather in Cain's view of greatness.

To Cain, greatness could be accomplished with very little personal sacrifice. Yet, Abel understood that the requirements of greatness are requirements which are defined by God and not by Abel or Cain. Genesis 4:3-4 share a detail that most readers pass over. In these two verses we learn four dangers about allowing our children to pursue greatness based on comparing themselves to others. Let's learn from this.

*"And in process of time it came to pass, that Cain brought of the fruit of the ground an offering unto the Lord. And Abel, he also brought of the firstlings of his flock and of the fat thereof. And the Lord had respect unto Abel and to his offering:"*

**Danger #1: Comparing others may not always be wrong.**

We discover in verse 3 that Cain was comparing himself to Abel over a process of time. This allowed for a hatred to brew inside the heart of Cain. But we do not read in the Bible that Cain started with a hatred for his brother. The hatred grew during a "process of time" as the Bible states.

My oldest daughter, Jada, enjoys gymnastic classes. There are many talented girls at more advanced levels than my daughter. On a ride home she once said, "Dad, Bethany is the best gymnast in our class."

As a parent, there are several ways I could have tackled that statement.

"You know, I heard she has a terrible home life. I've talked to her pastor and he tells me that she is miserable at home. You are much better off." This is a response intended to build my daughter up by tearing down someone else's life. This is never a good idea. This type of response would have only helped to spark an ego within my daughter. An ego which knows secret faults about those with great talents and enjoys watching when the talented are hurting. Bad idea.

How about this one?

"You know, Bethany is great at gymnastics, but nobody is better than you at painting fingernails. And painting fingernails is much more likely to land you a real job here in town. And besides, what if she broke her leg? Then what? See, you could still paint fingernails with a broken leg." This response is intended to point out my daughter's other qualities and to somehow make them more exciting and practical. Fail.

I don't want my daughter to be holding the bat in the next Kerrigan/Harding scandal. Over time, this response would have my daughter waiting for some physical accident to happen to Bethany so that my daughter can say (as with me), "See, I told you so. What will poor Bethany do now?" So, what responses are left? Maybe, we should first ask ourselves some questions.

What are we trying to accomplish by giving our children a definite solution? What problem are we trying to solve? Why is it not OK for a child to be better in a skill than our children? Why do we, as parents, feel as though we have to run in and save our children from every unwanted or unpleasant emotion?

Here's how I responded to my daughter that day, "Bethany is very gifted in gymnastics. How does that make you feel?"

"I feel happy for her. Dad, she works hard and practices all the time. She deserves to make the team."

Do you see what just happened? It's something we parents never take the time to realize. My daughter was not upset at Bethany being better in gymnastic. She was actually happy for her and wanted to share it with me.

Parents, if we're not careful we can run into the burning house of our children's hearts, ready to douse the flames, only to realize there is no fire. And in turn, we unknowingly start a spark of hatred in our children's hearts. And over a "process of time" our children will never be Go-Getters for God with hatred buried deep within their thoughts.

## Danger #2: Ignoring the warning signs.

What amazes me about the account of Cain and Abel is the lack of Adam and Eve. Where were the parents while all this hatred and wrong comparison was taking place in Cain's heart? It is true we are not

told the exact age of Cain or Abel at the time of this event. But we do know that both lived very close to their parents, Adam and Eve.

I believe they could have very well been aware of Cain's improper feelings of comparison and hatred for Abel. Yet, we find no mention of the parents. If Mom and Dad were there, they simply ignored this feeling Cain had towards Abel.

If we discover our children speaking habitually about others being better or greater than they are, we had better not ignore this behavior. Often, it's a warning sign of a deeper issue which could be an indicator of low self-esteem. While others can be greater at tasks than our children, others are never more important to God or to us parents. If this attitude of improper comparison is left unattended it could lead to hatred forming in a child's heart.

## Danger #3: Comparing others could cause egotism.

We find a unique conversation in Genesis 4:6-7.

*"And the Lord said unto Cain, Why art thou wroth? and why is thy countenance fallen? If thou doest well, shalt thou not be accepted? and if thou doest not well, sin lieth at the door. And unto thee shall be his desire, and thou shalt rule over him."*

What makes this conversation unique is the people conversing. God is actually speaking with Cain and seems genuinely concerned with Cain's comparison.

One of the problems with our children comparing themselves to others is that self-evaluation gets turned off. Cain stopped evaluating his own offerings to God and started looking at Abel's offerings.

Cain's focus had shifted; he now looked for Abel to fail instead of looking at his own faults. If Cain would have stopped and evaluated his own motives, he would have seen what God saw. I don't believe Cain was angry just because his offering was not pleasing to God, but rather because Abel's offering was acceptable. This is why we find God asking Cain some questions which should have been easy for Cain to answer.

"Why are you angry? Why are you pouting? If you know to do good and you do it, do you think that I will not be pleased? Cain, be careful because sin is knocking at your heart's door."

Something blinded Cain from seeing the dirt of his own life. Egotism will cause a person's stupidity to be hidden from only that person! This is what egotism will do to a person who is constantly comparing others. Unfortunately for these brothers, Cain listened to his ego instead of listening to his God. And it all started with comparing.

## Danger #4: A Life of Competition is a Hard Life.

Instead of repenting to God and apologizing to Abel, Cain allowed his ego and his habit of comparing others to grow. Like hand-feeding a wild lioness, these beasts in Cain's mind quickly turned on him.

These dangers are very real in our children's minds as well. It's up to us, as parents, to watch for the warning signs and know how to act.

I think we would all agree, "Proud parent of an Egotistical Murderer" would make a lousy bumper sticker. Our children will never accomplish great things for God if they are not even aware of their own faults, which brings up another question. What if I have a child who sees herself as better than everyone else? Are there any Biblical examples of this? You betcha'.

The habit of comparing others to yourself is a dangerous two-way street. We have just looked at the danger of your children comparing themselves as less than others. But what about the other side of the road? What are the dangers in allowing our children to compare themselves to others who are less talented in certain areas than our children?

Reading through the New Testament will reveal one of Jesus' greatest challenges in his ministry. The challenge of hypocrisy. Allowing your child to compare themselves as being better than others will harbor a mentality of hypocrisy in their lives.

In the Bible, Jesus tells a story about a man who compared his prayer life with the prayer life of another. This man was a Pharisee and thought of himself as a much better prayer warrior than the Publican who was also praying that day. The Pharisee had all the right words, the right movements, the right wardrobe, and even a beautifully powerful voice. He was the Elvis Presley of Jewish Prayer Partners. His prayers were beautifully written and rehearsed. No doubt, everyone wanted to model their prayers after him.

In this Biblical passage found in Luke 18:10-14, I discovered three hazards of allowing our children to compare themselves as better than others.

### Hazard #1: Your Child Will Want to Always Be Noticed.

In this passage, Jesus tells us that two men prayed. One stood up for all to see while the other humbly fell on his face before God. The Pharisee wanted everyone to see him high and lifted up, especially compared to the Publican who was down on his knees. A habit of comparing others will cause a desire to crave attention. Not only will your child see herself as better, but she will want others to see it also.

Most days, around lunch time, I head out to our local park for my runs. After my runs, I always swing by the house to shower before heading back into the office. Abram, my four-year-old, is usually waiting at the door when I return. He's ready to run with gym shorts on, my old broken wrist watch (for GPS tracking) on his wrist, and a water bottle in his hand. These tools are essential for all the "miles" he will run.

As I pull in the driveway, Abram meets me in the front yard and begins his route which is made up of a path around two trees located in our front yard. Each of Abram's laps is about 20 feet in length. What I've noticed about Abram's running is his desire to be watched. When running, he pays more attention to me than to where he's heading. Remember what he runs around? Yep, two trees. Countless times he has almost run face-first into a tree.

You see, Abram wasn't running for himself. Abram was running for the attention he received from Daddy. While this is cute to see in a 4-year-old, the need to always be noticed isn't so cute in an 18-year-old. Never allow your child to compare himself to others in order to draw more attention to himself.

## Hazard #2: Your Child Will Fail to See His Own Faults.

This Pharisee had become very good at spotting the sins of others, yet never seeing his own act of comparison as a sin against God. Children who display this type of hazard in their lives will often have a difficult time complimenting others.

I enjoy cycling. It's a great way to exercise while enjoying some great conversations with my cycling buddies. The catch to having a conversation while cycling is that you have to stay together. Staying in a close group allows you to draft behind others and to move at a faster rate than if you were cycling by yourself.

Now, there is one cycling friend who never keeps up with the group. For the fear of this friend reading this book let's call him Bubba. Here in Tennessee, Bubba is a safe alias to use. Statistically, 38% of all Tennesseans are named Bubba and this includes females. I think I read that in an Ed Stetzer stat once.

Bubba, as we'll call him (or her), always lags behind the group. Always. We are a very kind cycling group, waiting on Bubba to catch up to us at each rest stop. And just like clockwork, once Bubba makes his way to the rest stop, he will begin with a long list of excuses for being so slow.

At first Bubba's excuses were accepted, but after a while the group could easily pick up on the habitual excuses. Bubba would blame all types of things for his slowness. He blamed everything except himself.

Here are some of Bubba's most popular excuses for his slowness: The wind, the heat, the cold, the humidity, the dinner from the night before (usually Mexican), the breakfast from the morning of, the air pressure in his tires, the gear components on his bike, the clothes he was wearing, the medication his was on once for an infection, the oncoming traffic, the neighborhood dogs (which oddly causes me to pedal faster!), the dirt in his eyes, the new bike seat, the helmet, the list goes on and on.

What's the real problem? We all know it. Bubba is as slow as a turtle in a pond full of molasses, but he would never admit it. Our children need to see their own faults. This will help then to better see their own sins when they become adults.

## Hazard # 3: Your Child Will Grow Up Unsatisfied.

Jesus tells us the point of His parable. The Pharisee compared himself as better than the Publican and therefore walked away unjustified and unsatisfied. Even though he thought he was the King of Prayers, once he got home to the privacy of his own house he felt unsatisfied.

The problem with allowing our children to compare themselves as greater than others will result in an unsatisfied life. The Publican humbly cried out to God and never once compared his heartfelt prayer to anyone else's. Jesus said that this man went home happy and justified.

Now it's time for a more personal question. What happens when *we* compare our children to others?

Years after her divorce, my mother harbored harsh feelings for what my father had done to his family. And really, who could blame her? My father's name became the catch-all target in our household discussions and family gatherings.

Today as a parent, I can understand the hurt and anger in my mother's heart. Sometimes the only avenue she had to vent her frustrations was by sharing her feelings with her children. But there is a line which is dangerous when crossed.

Many times when I was disobedient to my mother or acted in a way she disliked (yes, I realize this is a shock to some of you), she would discipline me by placing me in the same category as someone she was unpleased with.

"Kevin, you're acting just like your father." This comparison absolutely defeated me. For years I had heard nothing but anger towards my father. So, to be compared to him was heartbreaking.

I must add some good news here. Years later my parent's relationship would be mended and they would become good friends. They even call each other from time to time just to chat. I'm very proud of the dad my father has become. God has allowed our relationship as father and son to become strong in the Lord. He really is a great dad and grandfather. It's as if God has restored all those years which the locust had eaten (Joel 2:25).

So take note: Allowing an attitude of comparisons to float in our children's hearts will lead to many dangers and hazards in their lives. It is a two way street with both ways leading to a disaster. As a parent, the best mentality to teach your child is to "Stare but Don't Compare."

Let's teach our children to show a life of greatness and how it looks when lived out

# Chapter Recap

**DO**:

- Allow your children to talk about the good qualities and talents of others.
- Ask your children questions about how other's talents make them feel.
- Teach your child to be confident in his or her own skills.
- Heed the Dangers and Hazards warned about in this chapter.

**DO NOT:**

- Compare your child to someone who is skilled less or more than your child.
- Allow your child to focus on someone's talent.
- Allow your child to envy others because of talents or skills they may display.

# CHAPTER 9
## Great in Their Authenticity

"And what sort of lives do these people, who pose as being moral, lead themselves? My dear fellow, you forget that we are in the native land of the hypocrite." - Oscar Wilde

As a child there was one horror movie which would terrify me every time I watched it. The scenes were gruesome. The evil characters were wicked. Sleep would run and hide from me on those nights. This movie is entitled *The Wizard of Oz*.

I think this movie was written by a father who wanted to scare the pudding out of his rebellious child. For many frightened viewers it was those evil flying monkeys. For others it was that ugly green-skinned witch. But for me, it was the image of the wicked witch's sister's feet when Dorothy's house landed on top of her. The way those feet curled and rolled up like the deflating of a child's blowout toy at a birthday party gives me chills as I type.

As horrifying as this movie is and as much as it made me want to never run away from home or crawl under a house, *The Wizard of Oz* has many parallels to the profession of Parenting. Sometimes as a parent you will feel like Dorothy: just a kid at heart, traveling down an unknown road and wanting to click your heels, making life normal again. When it comes to parenting, I sometimes feel like the brainless scarecrow because while I'm the one writing a book on parenting, I still have so much to learn.

Out of all the characters of *The Wizard of Oz*, I'll tell you who I resemble the most in my parenting. It's the Wizard. I'm often expected to be the great and powerful, but I'm simply a man behind a curtain who has little figured out about this parenting stuff. I've heard that a person can read 10 books on any subject and she will become an expert on that subject. Maybe this works on "How to write a query letter", but this rule does not apply to the subject of parenting. Maybe it's 10 books per child?

The point is, you will often see yourself as a person behind the curtain who's trying to look more together than you actually are, but to your children you are their great and powerful parent.

Because of this truth you must be their leader and you must lead in an authentic way. While many Christians can think a great deal on how to act as a Christian it might be more beneficial to take an alternate path in demonstrating how to live an authentic Christianity. Let's instead look at ways we can fake our Christianity.

To be honest, I didn't come up with this idea on my own. Jesus taught this in one of his most powerful parables. It's found in Matthew 25:1-13.

*"Then shall the kingdom of heaven be likened unto ten virgins, which took their lamps, and went forth to meet the bridegroom. And five of them were wise, and five were foolish. They that were foolish took their lamps, and took no oil with them: But the wise took oil in their vessels with their lamps. While the bridegroom tarried, they all slumbered and slept. And at midnight there was a cry made, Behold, the bridegroom cometh; go ye out to meet him.*

*Then all those virgins arose, and trimmed their lamps. And the foolish said unto the wise, Give us of your oil; for our lamps are gone out. But the wise answered, saying, Not so; lest there be not enough for us and you: but go ye rather to them that sell, and buy for yourselves. And while they went to buy, the bridegroom came; and they that were ready went in with him to the marriage: and the door was shut. Afterward came also the other virgins, saying, Lord, Lord, open to us. But he answered and said, Verily I say unto you, I know you not. Watch therefore, for ye know neither the day nor the hour wherein the Son of man cometh."*

In this parable Jesus shows us three ways someone can fake a Christian lifestyle. I'll stop typing now to let you read this parable because I know you skipped over the above scripture. Go ahead. I'll be here when you return. I need a coffee break anyway. I take a maximum of four coffee breaks a day. I couldn't stand to be away from it any longer than that.

You back? Good.

No doubt, this is a bizarre parable. It's bizarre to us because we are not a custom to the way weddings were performed at that time. So, it would help us to understand the order or process of how a traditional Jewish wedding would have been in the days of Christ.

If we don't know about their wedding ceremonies, it will be hard to understand the meaning of this parable. There was a little girl at a wedding who asked, "Mom, why do brides always wear white?"
The mom replied, "Because they're happy, dear."

Halfway through the wedding the girl whispered, "Mom, if all the brides wear white because they're happy, then why do all the men wear black?"

So, It would help us to know the ceremonies of that time. In the days of Christ, the Bridegroom would leave his parent's house and walk in a parade to *claim* his wife from her parents. The "virgins" would be part of this parade. The Bridegroom would then walk back with his wife to their new house. The Bridegroom's house is where the actual wedding ceremony would take place.

After the wedding ceremony, the Bridegroom and Bride would travel back to the Bride's parent's house and the Bridegroom would provide a three day celebration at the Bride's parent's home. You still tracking? Under these traditions we can begin to see that Jesus gives this parable as a warning.

It's a warning to the phonies. Those who are lost but are pretending to be saved. This parable is for the Apostate who comes and worships with us every Sunday and has us all fooled. In this parable Jesus reveals three ways to fake Christianity.

## Ways to Fake Christianity #1: Carry a big stick.

By studying the parables for an entire year as I preached them to our church congregation, I have learned that Jesus' parables are very symbolic. The Greek word used in this parable for "virgins" is Parthenos which means a bride's maid. And in this ceremony, the Bride's maids would be the ones responsible for illuminating the party. This is why they all had, what the Bible calls, "lamps". But this is not a small nightstand lamp which would be of very little help to a large crowd in the dark. These lamps were what we would call a torch on a long poll. Think Indiana Jones. Now, the foolish ones, or phonies, had the same equipment as the wise. They all had big sticks or torches that were to shine in order for others to see the Bridegroom in the dark. The lamps are symbolic of the Word of God.

The phony Christians will carry the same big stick that the real Christians carry. They may be lost but they know the scriptures. They may be lost but they enjoy coming to church. They may be lost but they proudly carry their bible. Therefore, we have to teach our children that Christianity is more than knowing the scriptures, attending church, or carrying all the Christian gear. It's about a personal relationship with Christ.

There was something different between the wise and the foolish. The wise had oil and the foolish thought they would not need any oil. The oil in this parable is symbolic of the Holy Spirit of God. The

wise knew that the oil would help the lamp burn brighter and longer. Without the oil the flame would not last. There are some phony Christians today who have once burned brightly but for a short moment in time and then it was revealed that the Holy Spirit was not within them.

Have you ever wondered how a person could sit under biblical preaching and godly worship and not be moved or convicted? Have you ever wondered why a person would just stop going to a church and never desire to be around God's people? It could be that they are faking this Christian stuff. But they carry the same equipment as real Christians. Teaching our children the Christian way is great, but we must not forget to teach them the Christian meaning. To our children, Christianity has to mean more than just carrying a large Christian torch around.

## Ways to Fake Christianity # 2: Work as hard as the true Believers.

The foolish or phonies tried their best to work and buy their own oil at the last minute. We should never build up this false idea in our children's minds that if they work hard enough for God or if they do enough good works then God will magically transform them into Christians. You nor I can never do enough good to make us Christians. That's why the cross of Jesus Christ is the only means of salvation that God will ever accept. As our children witness us doing Christian tasks, they should never see this as a means of salvation.

Our children need to understand that there is no person who could ever work enough to be forgiven. What's often confused is this: The true believers work for the Lord because we have *been* saved, not because we *want* to be saved. Christians work on the outside because Jesus has changed them on the inside. It's foolish to mutate this in our child's mind: To work on the outside with no change on the inside.

## Ways to Fake Christianity # 3: Proclaim that Jesus is Lord.

The phony Christians have no trouble proclaiming that Jesus is Lord, but there is more required than just this proclamation. The Bible teaches that even the demons know this much. It's also not enough to proclaim Jesus as a god or as a master. Jesus Christ must be proclaimed as *your* God and as *your* Master.

An easy way to read the spiritual temperature of your child is to ask him or her this question: "To *you*, who is Jesus?" Some may answer, "He is Lord and He is Savior." But most true Believers will answer, "He is *my* Lord and He is *my* savior" It's easy to proclaim that Jesus is Lord, but it's bolder to say, "Jesus is *my* Lord."

Let me give you an easy way to test your own salvation. Ask yourself this simple question concerning this parable: Who is doing the knocking in your heart and mind?

Who was doing the knocking in this parable? The Foolish. But if you read Revelation 3:20, you will find that Jesus is the one doing the knocking.

As a true Christian, I will never have to knock on a door to get to where Jesus is located. The Bible says I can come boldly to the throne room of God now that I am a Christian through the shed blood of Jesus Christ.

If you are the one doing the knocking, then you are on the wrong side of the door! And when the great Bridegroom comes for his Bride (the church) the door of God's grace will close.

You can carry your bible. You can work for Jesus. You can even proclaim His name. But if you have never repented of your sins and turned to Christ for your salvation, then you are not a Child of God. According to the Word of God, if you die in this state you will not be allowed to enter into Heaven and you will find yourself outside the gate.

So, the best way I can teach my children what an authentic Christian looks like is to be one myself. A genuine, blood-bought Christian who realizes daily the relationship with Man and God. This is the example of authenticity that all children need to model

themselves after. Don't teach your child how to fake a
Christian life by leading one yourself.

# Chapter Recap

**DO:**

- Hide your fear of the *Wizard of Oz.*
- Study the Parables of Christ. You will be blessed.
- Proclaim Christ as your Lord and Savior.
- Be your child's Great and Powerful.

**DO NOT:**

- Drink coffee all freaking day long.
- Be a fake Christian.
- Consider your good deeds as your salvation.
- Lead only by your good works.

# CHAPTER 10
## Great in Their Humility

### "Sorry, but your child stinks :( "

Humility. How in the world is a person to properly teach that? And, why is it so difficult to teach? Maybe the problem lies in the understanding of the very definition.

The word *humility* means to have a modest view of one's own importance. This is why it's difficult to teach. We humans will always have to fight a natural urge to elevate ourselves and our offspring. It's in our blood. Look around in this culture and you will find a people who are consumed with themselves and their own needs. And if we are not careful, we will unknowingly pass this trend of egoism on to our children.

We live in a day where every child gets a trophy even if they never make a play. Every child is a success even if they fail. Every child passes the class even if they have no clue how to comprehend the topic. Why are we afraid to allow our children to fail even at the small things? And who will our children become by growing up with a false sense of how to honestly self-evaluate?

I can't tell you how many good people I've seen fall morally because they never stopped to give themselves an honest self-evaluation. Many pastors have hurt their fellow church members, slept with multiple women, become addicted to drugs, and ruined their ministries all because of their fabricated hubris. By the way, hubris is not a bone in the human body.

Why are pastors so vulnerable to all the above sins? Because thousands of church members are often afraid to reveal to their pastor that he has areas which need improving. Basically, he stinks in some ways. He is praised so much that he will soon start seeing his sins as almost deserving and acceptable to God.

As a preacher, if I'm stinking it up in an area of my ministry, I want to know! I don't want to continue to think that I'm knocking it out of the park when, in fact, I'm striking out each and every time at bat. A person will never improve in a task if they believe they are doing the task perfectly.

I hate to be the one to break this to you, but your child is not perfect. As a matter of fact you child is so imperfect that a perfect God had to come to this earth and die for your child's sins. Yep, it's that bad. So, the best way to teach humility is to demonstrate it to your child.

When it comes to humility, I'm still learning how to have and show more of it. So, it's quite difficult for me to teach, but this is no excuse not to try and be open for the moments when God wants us to grow in our humility so that we can share it with our children. And rest assured, if you are willing to look, God will provide the moments. He did this with me one day through Keith.

Keith was a homeless man walking down the highway my office is located on. He was struggling under the weight of carrying two backpacks and a large rolled up tarp. It was cold that day and difficult to walk with no shoulder to separate him from the seventy miles-per-hour cars zooming past. You could almost see the force of the passing cars attempting to spin his backpack from off his shoulders. It was eleven in the morning and he already looked as if he would pass out at any moment. It was not for show because he didn't know I was watching and studying him.

Before I became a Christian, I would have probably rolled down my window and shouted, "Get a job, you bum!"

But now that I have the God of the universe beating inside my heart a different emotion filled my mind. I can't label it compassion nor would I call it pity. The feeling was more like a duty. Something that I should do just because it would be the right thing to do. It's one of those moments when you know that turning away would be a sin to you.

He looked shocked and carried an eye of suspicion as I opened my Jeep's passenger door. I told him I was heading towards the interstate if he wanted a ride. I was expecting him to jump right in but he studied me for a moment, nodded his head, and dropped the backpacks from off his shoulders. Before climbing into the cab, he offered his hand.

"My name's Keith."

"Glad to meet you, Keith. I'm Kevin."

We both smiled as he tossed his bags in the back and southbound we went.

Along the six mile route little was spoken except small talk about the weather and his previous locations. It didn't take long for the cab to fill with the smell of a dirty dumpster, but Keith never apologized. He would never label himself as a homeless man. Keith preferred the caption of a Traveler. He was proud of his latest find - a pair of shoes which he pulled out of a Gallatin dumpster last night before bedding down in the wet grass just behind the Post Office. To my surprise the shoes looked as though they had just came off a shoe store shelf.

With no family alive anymore save an older brother in California, Keith admitted to always having a wandering spirit ever since childhood. Always curious about what's around the corner, Keith was well schooled in how to survive in his non-paying traveling profession.

My stomach growled and I asked Keith if he wanted to grab a bite to eat before we reached the interstate. My treat. I could sense a hesitation in his body language. There's no telling how long it's been since he's had a full and warm meal. I asked why the caution about eating with me but he quickly changed the subject to his hometown in Oklahoma. Odd.

As the bustle of the I-40 exit came into view, the smell of the surrounding restaurants started to quickly leak through the canvas top of my Jeep. His hunger was visible yet he refused a free meal. So I asked why.

Keith told me about the last man who offered to give him a ride and a warm meal. The driver picked Keith up, pulled into a gas station, and told Keith to go inside and get whatever food he wanted while the driver pumped some gas in his truck. You could see the pain in Keith's eyes as he then told of looking out the store window and watching the driver pull off without Keith and with Keith's entire life belongings. Keith was a veteran traveler and he was cautious of me.

I assured him that we would sit and eat together. "Besides," I told him, "your clothes won't fit me." He didn't find that funny.

As we pulled into the restaurant's parking lot Keith admitted that he wasn't dressed to eat inside. So, I looked in the back of my Jeep and found a blue Titans tee-shirt and tossed it towards him. I could see his thankfulness through his smile.

Before we entered through the storefront doors

Keith stopped and took his hat off. Once inside he wanted me to order first, then he ordered the exact same. I didn't realize it at the time but Keith probably had trouble reading the menu.

When our meals came, I asked Keith if I could pray for our food and for his travels. He smiled revealing his tarred and offset teeth. After my prayer, Keith dropped his guard and started a conversation about prayer and faith.

"I guess because you prayed, you are a Christian?"

"Yep. I sure am."

"So, is that why you picked me up?"

I had to think about this one.

"Yes and No. I picked you up because I would want to be picked up, so No. But Yes, because if it were not for Jesus changing my life I would have probably tried to see if I could run you into the ditch." Again, Keith didn't laugh.

He had never had a gyro with lamb meat and he ate like he would never have another.

"You're not like most Christians I've met."

"How's that, Keith?"

"Usually they will only help me out in order to witness to me, or hand me a tract, or try to convert me to their religion or denomination. Once they see I'm not interested, they're done with helping a traveler like me out."

"That's sad."

"Why are you different? Do you have any tracts?"

"Nope."

"Are you scared to share the Gospel with me?"

"I don't think so." I said with a smile, since I hadn't yet told Keith I was a Pastor.

"Well, aren't you going to share the Gospel with me?"

"Do I need to?"
This question puzzled Keith. For the first time since we met, Keith laughed allowing a small piece of lamb meat to fall onto his untrimmed beard. His answer was priceless.

"No. I'm a Christian myself. Been saved for almost 30 years and I do love my Lord. Was baptized in the river. One of the greatest days of my life. Of all these years of traveling nobody's ever asked me about my faith. They just assume that I'm a sinful lost homeless bum."

"Keith, I would call you more of a Traveler." We both smiled at each other as we continued sipping our Sprites.
After the meal, I helped Keith with his bags. Still, he was very guarded over his belongings. He started to take off the shirt I loaned him earlier but I told him he could keep it. As we shared a big man hug with each other, I told Keith how far Nashville was from where we were and told him I've got one more thing for him.
I reached into my wallet and handed Keith one of my business cards. I told him to call me if he ever needed prayer or help. He held the card just inches from his nose and studied it for a good while. You

could see his mouth trying to sound out the word pastor.

He looked up at me with tears in his eyes and asked, "You're a pastor?"

"Yes. I am."

"No," Keith insisted, "today, you were an angel sent from God."

I smiled in reply, "No, Keith. Today, *you* were the angel."

Keith's final words to me were, "Brother, I'll see you on the other side of this world. When you sit and think about it, Kevin, I suppose we are all travelers on this small thing called Earth."

With that, Keith gave me the most curious wink as if he was radiating the glow of God Himself.

As I drove back to my office, the aroma of trash still lingered in the cab but that didn't keep me from praising God. And to think, I almost missed a great blessing by not stopping to help a fellow traveler out.

I wonder how many Messengers we have passed by. How many Brothers or Sisters we have missed out on having wholesome conversations? How many travelers we have tried to push our religion on without first showing them the love of Christ and getting to know them?

So, if you get to heaven before me and see an angel in a blue Titans shirt, will you please tell Keith I said hi? Thanks.

In the presence of Keith, I had a lesson on humility. Later that night at the dinner table I shared my story about Keith with my family. You could see in my children's eyes the realization that all humans are.. well... human. It's one thing to say we are humble but it becomes another creature when we start to implement humility in our actions.

## Humility is hard to teach for a reason.

For me, humility is so hard to teach because I so often fail at showing it. Maybe you're like me - getting caught up in your schedule, your life, your plans, your tasks, your responsibilities, your, your, your. And before you realize it, you've acted like a jerk to someone simply because you failed to be humble. Let me share with you an embarrassing story.

The line was crazy long, which should come as no surprise considering it was just a week till Christmas. Being impatient, I decided to park and go inside to place my coffee order instead of waiting in the line. As I turned my Jeep off, I glanced at the last car in line and made it a mental game to see if I could come back out with my coffee before that car made it to the ordering speaker.

An easy win for me knowing that most of the time I'm waiting in line behind people who order fifteen different additives to their drinks. I get tired just listening to them order. I can't imagine having to fulfill such demands. Me? Black and straight. That's how coffee comes. That's how God intended coffee to be. My order takes three seconds to fill.

As I came through the storefront doors, I was glad to see only one person standing in my way of a caffeinated victory. I took my place in line behind a woman and I noticed by her stare at the menued wall that she was undecided. No big deal. I glanced out the window and could still see the car I was racing hadn't moved. But then the tide began to turn.

This woman in front of me continued to just stand there, staring at the menu. I shot my eyes at the barista and he didn't seem to mind the wait. So, I just stuck my hands in my pockets and let out a quiet huff. I'm a professional huffer by the way, just ask my wife.

The wait felt like an eternity. Then the cars began to move in the line outside. I could almost see the grill on the front of the car smiling at me and my soon-to-be defeat. So, I decided to help nudge this woman along in her decision making.

I started with the polite cough to alert her that I've been back here waiting for an eternity. Nothing. So, I moved on to the side-to-side sway mingled with a standard pee-pee dance and occasional wristwatch glancing. Still, nothing. To make matters worse, this undecided woman reached deep into her jacket pocket, pulled out her phone, and started to stare now at her screen. Unbelievable!

I looked at the barista again with a look as if I'd been kidnapped and I needed him to call 911. But he returned my stare with a look of disgust. I was confused. Why was the barista upset with me when this woman with a phobia of coffee-ordering was wasting my time?

I was getting frustrated as I could no longer see the car I was competing with. I couldn't believe I was going to lose because of this uncommitted woman. But the straw that broke the back of my politeness was when she started to text on her phone. So I blurted out, "Good grief!" and gave one of the greatest huffs I've ever huffed in my huffing career.

About four other baristas then turned in unison and shot cold stares right at me. If it hadn't been a group of baristas, I would have been worried I was about to get a beat-down. Was this woman their family? A coworker? I didn't understand. And to top it all off, the car I was racing just pulled up to the drive thru window, got their coffee, and drove off leaving me standing in line defeated and confused.

At that moment, as I was about to turn and leave in frustration, this woman, who had caused me such great humiliation and defeat, handed the barista her phone. He smiled politely at her as he gently took her phone, and read her order while pecking on his screen. He handed back her phone as she tried to mutter the words "Thank you" which sounded more like a long and awkward grown.

What I had not taken the time to realize is that this woman was deaf and mute. She was simply typing in her order on her phone. What she didn't know was what a big jerk I had been behind her back, but others saw my hissy fit.

It's a humbling thing to have to call to order the entire coffee shop and publicly apologize for not showing humility, patience, and compassion. As I paid for both of our orders, it cost me a lot more than $4.32. It cost me my pride and my dignity. Learn from me: If we start every interaction with humility, we will never have to end with it.

**Humility can be taught anywhere/anytime.**

Another way we can show a great humility is in the area of our children's sports and activities. Because we take great ownership in our children, we can often be too overpowering on the field and none of us want to be the *weird* parent which other parents whisper about. If we don't learn some good tips, then we may one day hear our child scream, "Stop it! You're not my coach!"

It continues to be my goal as a father of seven to be a life-coach with dreams of my children growing up to be great leaders, one or two United States Presidents, and (of course) a couple of Billy Grahams. I try to teach my children the important things in life like love, good manners, and the truth about coconuts (they are not really nuts). I experience great joy in conversations with my children about their interests and sports. So, the sentence "You're not my coach!" can blindside a parent like me.

I quickly discovered I could not coach my children from the sidelines without sending mixed signals. Here are 10 tips to help master the Parent-Coach Balance:

1.    **You're the parent, not the coach.** If you want to be the coach, sign-up! Most childhood-sport organizations are always looking for volunteer coaches and assistants.

2.    **Wear the proper jersey.** Your child is probably more nervous than you. It's best to wear your "encourage" jersey instead of your "run harder" jersey. I once asked my oldest son what he liked the best about playing baseball. He answered, "I like to look in the stands and see you smiling at me." (Instant dad-tears)

3.    **Put on your game face.** Don't be rude. Watch your child during practices and games instead of burying your head in a book or phone.

4.    **Play by the rules.** Don't bite the fence in two with fear of your child being hit by a stray ball. While there is some danger in playing any sport, coaches should have your child's safety at the top of the list.

5.    **Don't adopt the Empty Nester Syndrome.** Your child is on the field by himself, not driving off to college. Enjoy the fact that he is stepping out on his own but not in total independence of your parenting.

6.    **Leave the bullhorn.** Yelling at games is expected. However, the coach may frown upon yelling *at* your child. If a play was fouled-up because of your child, ask yourself: Does the coach or my child realize the cause? If you can answer "yes", then yelling at your child will be redundant and hurtful.

7. **Your child is not your re-incarnation.** She may have a different speed or endurance level than you remember having when you were a child. Don't try to make her the athlete you were not.

8. **Don't be a step-coach.** While practicing at home in the backyard with your child, reinforce what the coach taught, even if you don't completely agree.

9. **Your child is on a team.** Never encourage him to be a one-man show. While on a team, your child should learn more about teamwork than about his athletic abilities.

10. **Give the coach a smile.** Most coaches are also parents trying to juggle a job, family, and sports. A simple nod of approval or word of encouragement could be all the coach needs to become a better leader.

If you really want to feel like the Coach, then be the Coach of Organization.

1. Lead the <u>Snack Support</u> – Within the first few practices help to organize a game snack rotation for the parents.

2. Lead the <u>Caravan</u> – Build the team moral by organizing a caravan to the games.

3. Lead the <u>Huddle</u> – Make sure to sit with other parents during practices with the intent of making new friendships.

4. Lead the <u>Celebration</u> - Help organize the end of the season party. By this time the coaches are exhausted and the last thing on their mind is gathering the team, parents, and volunteers for a party. This is a great way for you to take a huge load off the coaches

# Chapter Recap

## DO:

- Look for ways to demonstrate humility.
- Grow in your own humility as a parent.
- Try a gyro with lamb meat. They are delicious.
- Help your child on their field of sports by showing humility.

## DO NOT:

- Pick up travelers if they are holding an axe.
- Think that your child is the perfect one. There is only One perfect and it isn't your child.
- Associate humility with weakness. They are miles apart from each other.
- Be a jerk. Ever. If you start with humility, you won't have to end with it.

# CHAPTER 11
## Great in Their Service

**"Anybody can be great because anybody can serve others." - Martin Luther King Jr.**

The main thing that will show your child's greatness will be in their service to others. This is important to realize, because if your child fails to learn how to serve others then his or her greatness will not be that great.

What is the meaning of service? Why do we serve? What does genuine service look like? Let me illustrate the meaning of true service by sharing with you an event that showed me a great definition of service.

My wife and I enjoy taking our family to a restaurant called the Spaghetti Factory, which is located on 2nd Avenue in downtown Nashville. One evening after a wonderful meal at this restaurant, we prepared to walk back to the parking garage located on 4th Avenue. Since it was now dark, I took a few minutes to warn my young children about some of the things they might see on the streets of downtown Nashville. I instructed all of them to stay close to Mom or Dad and not to talk to anyone, especially the street peddlers.

As we stepped past the restaurant doors, it was worse than I'd envisioned. The bars were now open, the street musicians were playing, and the beggars were out in teams.

Of course in this setting, our large family stuck

out like a plumber's backside. So, we didn't even make it to the street corner before a beggar made his way to my children. What happened next not only shocked me but also taught me a lesson I'll never forget.

The beggar had his sights locked on one of my daughters, Ella, who was around five-years-old at this time and smiled at everything her eyes looked upon. As the beggar got closer I noticed he had something in his right hand. I wouldn't call it a floral bouquet. It looked more like a handful of wilted chigger weeds.

When he made it to our small street corner herd, he bent down towards my daughter. My Daddy Security Radar was on high alert but I held back, being just as curious as my children. With a smile, this thinly, dirty, and smelly man handed my daughter one of his wilted flowers and said, "Jesus loves you."

He proceeded to repeat this process for each of our children. After he was done, he straightened his tired back, looked me square in the eyes with a wrinkled smile, and walked his torn sandals back down the sidewalk. He didn't ask for money. He didn't ask for food. He didn't even ask for a "thank you." I realized he gave all his flowers to my children. Flowers he probably picked to be sold that night. Absolute humility covered over my heart but God, with His wonderful sense of humor, was not yet done with me.

The light changed and we proceeded to cross the street in a hurried fashion and walked into the parking garage. Out of the corner of my eye I saw him come around the corner and stagger toward us. Another beggar.

Surely my earlier lecture in the restaurant would prove true with this visibly drunk man. He was heading right for us like a dive-bomber bent on imploding our walking huddle. So, I took the lead and prepared to push him away if our courses were to collide.

Just when I thought of putting my hands up and bracing for an impact, the man stopped, stepped to the side, and tipped the brim of his inside-out hat. In passing, I heard him slur, "Good day, Sir." And with that, he politely continued down the street in his swayed gait.

When we reached our vehicle and got buckled in, I had to apologize to my family. I had taught them to fear and ignore people who are simply in a tough spot in their lives. That night was one of my most Pharisaical moments. I then taught them what God had just taught me.

These two beggars showed us more compassion and politeness than I even thought about showing them. I would drive away. They would walk. I would sleep that night on a soft bed and in a secured home. They would sleep on the pavement, open and exposed. We had just eaten more food in one meal than those two beggars will eat all week long.

Yet despite the vast difference in lifestyles that night, they were more like Jesus than I was. They demonstrated faith, kindness, and love to total strangers while I demonstrated bitterness mixed in a big bowl of hubris. One day I hope to meet these two beggars again so that I might repay them for their kindness to my family.

I now teach my children to see people not for what they appear to be in our eyes but for what they appear to be in the eyes of Christ. And where did I learn such a valuable lesson? Well, from a couple of beggars... where else?

This is the true definition of service: The ability to see people the same way God sees people. This should be what motivates you to serve. When we do this we will become some of the best servants God could ask for. I beg to argue that this is why we don't see a lot of selfless service in today's world.

We have been blinded by our own ambitions, wants, and needs. And we have failed to see people for what they are in desperate need of. If we truly realized all the many ways we influence our children, we would probably monitor our influencers more closely. While there are many influencers we could list, I want to give you four of my main ones.

## The Influence of Leadership.

The other day my kids and I were walking out of Wal-Mart and they took the lead but they forgot where we parked. I told them, "Don't lead if you don't know where you're going." We have enough of that in America today. Many say even our government is a good example of leading without knowing where you're going. Parents have to know where they're going in this world because they are leading their children. Maybe there was a time in your life when you had to turn away from following one or both of your parents. You had to turn from their leadership in fear of ending up just like them. Maybe you've said as a child, "When I grow up I'm not gonna be anything like them."

I don't ever want my children to one day say, "I had to turn away from following my dad."

So how do we lead in a way that our children will want to follow in our footsteps? Let me share with you three techniques that are great to follow.

**#1: Always do what is right**, even when others don't. That great ark builder, Noah, did what was right even though nobody else did. Read Genesis, chapter 6 and 7.

**#2: Always lead more by your actions** and less by your Words. Just look at the example that Joshua set for his family and his people. Read Joshua 24:14-16.

**#3: Always be passionate** for what you believe in. King David was an awesome leader because of his passion. Read 1 Samuel 17:45-51.

I hope that my children see my passion for God and that they will follow after that same passion and zeal. We must never forget that all parents will influence their children with leadership.

**The Influence of <u>Burdens</u>.**

When trouble comes your way, you had better believe that your children are watching how you will react. It's easy to talk about having joy and peace that surpasses all understanding. But when you are faced with devastation, then it all becomes painfully real. No doubt, your children will be influenced by how you react to life's challenges and burdens.

How will your children see you react when your job asks you to transfer into a strange city? How will your children see you react when you lose your spouse? How will your children see you react when the doctor tells you it's cancer? Through our burdens we are still able to influence our children in a positive way.

As a parent, I want to share with you a frightening reality: children will often carry great burdens that originated with the parents. Let me give you an example of how this works. Often in a divorce a child will feel as if he or she was the reason for the divorce. "Why do they do that?", you may ask. Because they are influenced by the burden of the parents during the divorce.

Someone once truthfully stated, "Our children watch us the most when we are under pressure." You better be sure that your children are watching your reactions when burdens arrive at your door. Parents will influence with their burdens.

## The Influence of **Friends**.

You and I have been born into a certain family. I can't change that. You can't change that. We all have crazies in our family. Maybe a crazy uncle, cousin, or grandpa. Maybe some days *you* feel like the crazy in the family. But the one thing we can control is who we chose to be our friends and those we let influence us.

When we birth our children, we place them among our friends. Our children have no say so in that matter. That's why it's important to be aware of who we make our friends and our people, because our children will also be influenced by them. The Israelites were terrible about this. They would move into a new land and make friends with people who worshipped strange gods. When the Israelite children grew up, they started worshiping the false gods that their parent's friends worshiped.

What we fail to realize as parents is that our children get influenced every day by the people we choose to hang out with. I'm so glad that God has placed my family in the middle of a great church family. What a great influence they all have been on my children! It's one of the great benefits of having a good church family. It's an influence that your children might not get from their own blood family.

My church family has made such an impact on me and my wife that we have written in our will that if anything happens to me and her, there is a couple in the church that we want to raise our children.

When I shared this Will Request from the pulpit to our church family everyone looked at each other like they were contestants in the Hunger Games. Every adult in that auditorium was silently praying this prayer, "Dear Lord, don't let the Pastor die before me."

But in all reality ask yourself this question, "If you were to die, would you be able to leave the care of your children to any of your friends?"

If not, then you might want to rethink who you allow to influence your children. Never forget that parents will always influence with their friends.

### The Influence of Faith.

What every child needs to understand from their parents' faith is this truth: While the Law of God *excludes* us from God's family because of sin, the grace of God *includes* us in God's family, if we put our faith and trust in Jesus Christ as our Lord and Savior. This

God of love and grace will sound foreign to your child if you have no faith as a parent. The influence of your faith will draw your child to Jesus, even if they don't completely understand Him. Even if they can't completely comprehend Him. Your faith will influence your child towards your God. Friend, the influence of a parent is one of the greatest powers you will ever possess. So, let me ask you, "How are you using this great power?"

# Chapter Recap

**DO:**

- Be passionate in your leadership towards your children.
- Visit the Spaghetti Factory in downtown Nashville.
- Remember that your children are watching how you react to the burdens and trials of your life.

**DO NOT:**

- Ignore the power of influence that your friends have over your children.
- Ever pick chigger weeds.
- Judge a person by their dress or the category you mentally place them in.

# CONCLUSION AND FINAL WORDS

Well, you made it! You have read this entire book! In honor of your success I want to give you a free cookie.*

I know there were times of doubt and remorse but you finished strong. It's my honest prayer that this book has helped you in your parenting. If you were convicted to the point of repentance and conversion to Christianity I would love to know. I like to pray for all those that I've helped along their Christian walk. You can email me the good news at Kevin@parentingthegreats.com

Until we meet again in our next journey together, stay strong because those kids are smarter than you think!

*Cookies are not redeemable while participant is on planet earth.*

# CONNECT WITH THE AUTHOR

You can find Kevin at his fan page on Facebook and get all of the latest updates on future books and speaking engagements. Just search for Kevin Butler – Christian Author and Speaker.

You can follow Kevin on Twitter at:
http://twitter.com/brokevin

Be sure to visit the website of *Parenting The Greats* at:
http://parentingthegreats.com

CPSIA information can be obtained at www.ICGtesting.com
Printed in the USA
LVOW01s1408160514

386127LV00012B/164/P

9 781493 640867